MANIPULATION AND DARK PSYCHOLOGY

How to Learn and Defend Yourself from Stop Being Manipulated and Protect Your Mind. Dark Psychology Secrets, Learn the Practical Uses and Defenses yourself.

BY BRANDON TRAVIS

Introduction

L earning the secrets of dark Psychology couldn't be done without understanding a little bit about the history and machinations of Psychology itself. It's thanks to pioneers like Carl Jung that we can come to terms with the dark side of our psyche, or our "shadow" as he named it.

In turn, you'll learn about tactics of dark Psychology including emotional manipulation, dark persuasion, and the long con. Once a foundation of dark Psychology has been established, this book moves on to mind control, brainwashing, and persuasion. Learn how to identify mind control and brainwashing in the media, and how this correlates with dark psychology. Then there are the dark persuaders out there – learn how to identify their techniques and unmask them.

And though everyone likes being seduced and has a hard time saying "no" when it seems like the perfect romantic partner comes along, there are dark seducers out there, too. This book will engage in the basics of dark seduction and some of the most popular techniques of influencing an individual to go home with you at night.

Dark Psychology is a tough, unwieldy subject. It can be used wisely, and it can be used for selfish, evil ends. We'll discuss how the dark triad of narcissism, Machiavellianism, and Psychopathy make an individual more likely to abuse the knowledge dark Psychology has to offer, and what techniques each type of person is prone to using.

Finally, learn how to protect yourself. It's one thing to know how to wield the secrets of dark psychology, but it's another to have someone stronger and more practiced use it on you. You'll learn how to identify how you've chosen to become the victim of a dark Psychology user and how to push back.

Chapter 1 - What Is Dark Psychology?

The idea with this one is that everyone, even if they realize it or not, will have the potential, if it is going to benefit themselves and even their families enough, to victimize other humans and creatures. Some people are just more willing to do it than others. For example, you may not think about doing this to just get a promotion at work or to get someone to notice you, but you may be willing to hurt other people if you knew it would save your life or save the life of someone in your family.

While many of us are going to restrain or hide this kind of tendency, there are those who are going to see these impulses and decide to act on them. The idea of dark psychology is to seek to understand these perceptions, feelings, thoughts, and even the subjective processing systems that tend to lead to the predatory behavior that is seen as unethical to what most of modern society is going to see as normal or good.

Dark psychology is going to assume that any abusive, deviant, or criminal behaviors that are showing up are done for a purpose. They may be seen as bad or evil, but the other person is doing them for some purpose, and not just because they feel like it. They are going to have a rational goal most of the time. Someone may use abuse to keep their partner in their place to ensure that they are able to get the love and attention that they need. Is this something that the majority of society would do or see as normal? No, but it is a rational excuse in the mind of the person doing it.

First, we need to take a look at how we are able to examine and identify the Dark Side when we look at psychological thought and behavior. We need to have some kind of measure in place to know what is normal and what is abnormal behavior for humans. The first measure of this is going to be social norms. The social norms are going to be any of the behaviors that society considers normal and a part of daily life.

We can also take a look at criminals. These individuals are often seen as some of the rejects of society because they often don't have the best upbringing and may not have learned the laws and societal norms like the rest of us. Yet in society, the largest harm is not going to be from these criminals with poor backgrounds. Instead, it is going to come from CEO's who embezzle and use theft, along with government officials. This kind of white collar crime often happens without most of us have any idea, and we end up missing out on some of it because it is hard to detect as well.

No, that we have taken a bit of time to take a look at these different types of crimes quickly we need to take a look at what psychology is going to say about this. What is brought up in psychology to help us talk about these deviants who do not see the actions they use as a problem and who feel that others who do not take control of their lives are weak, and because of this weakness, they deserve to become the victim in the scenario?

There are several thoughts that have come up with this. Some people may use it because they have not been taught from a young age what acceptable behavior is. Some people do it as a more evolutionary manner; the stronger should be able to take over those who are weaker. And some are going to use it as a way to help them survive the world because they see it as something that is harsh, and something that they need to be able to control on their own as well.

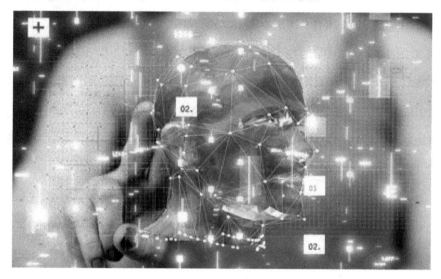

So, when we are taking a look at dark psychology, we are looking basically at the study of a human condition as it is going to relate on our psychological nature of people to prey upon one another for their own benefit. All of humanity really does have this potential in order to do this, although most of us are able to subdue this part of our subconscious and we aim to try and be better than this. While most of us are going to be able to sublimate or restrain this kind of tendency, there are times when people are going to react, and this is when some issues are going to show up.

Dark psychology is going to assume that this production is purposive and has some motivation that is driven by rationale and by goals in the process, at least 99.99 percent of the time. The rest of the time, this dark psychology is going to be a really brutal form of victimization of others, without having a good intent or any real good reason that it is being used in the first place.

The ideas that come with dark psychology are sometimes hard for us to hear about. It is going to assume that all of us have some malevolent intent found in us, whether we use it or not. This is going to be the Dark Continuum. Some of us have fleeting moments that we are able to hide behind and not use, and others are going to find that it is a lot harder and more obtrusive. Mitigating factors acting as attractions and accelerants to the dark singularity will determine how strong the malevolent intentions are and whether someone is going to be dealing with it at all.

Dark psychology is going to encompass all that will connect us to what is known as the dark side. All faiths, humanity, and cultures no matter how many rules and traditions that they have are going to have this dark side sometimes. From the moment that we are born to the time that we die, there is going to be a bit of this dark side found in us. We get to choose how we get to use it, and whether it is done just to cause harm to another person, or if it is done to help us progress with our goals and dreams.

Dark psychology believes that there are going to be people who are able to commit bad acts, say mean things, and they do it without any purpose. Most people will find that they are willing to do some things that may be found as horrible, but they will do it for sex, money, power, or something else in their lives. And then there are going to be those people who will do this without any known purpose in mind. They are going to commit a horrid act like this without having a goal. And these kinds of people are going to be the scariest ones of all. They do it because it brings them pleasure somehow, and not for any other reason.

To keep it simple, the ends are not going to justify the means for this kind of person. They are going to injure and violate those around them just because they can. There is a potential within all of us to cause this harm without reason, but most of us are able to stop ourselves before we get to this point because we want to follow the societal norms, and we have a sense of guilt and sorrow when we cause this kind of harm. Given the idea that most of us like to think that we are a more benevolent species, it would be easy to assume that we would have been able to move past these kinds of feelings and thoughts. However, this hasn't happened yet. All of us have had these thoughts at one point or another, even though most of us would not act upon them.

A few things that we need to look at quickly before we move on to some of the other aspects of dark psychology that are important include:

Dark psychology is going to be a condition that all humans are going to deal with. All societies, cultures, and more are going to have this condition, but there is a choice on whether or not to react to it.

This dark psychology is going to be the study of the human condition as it is going to relate to the perceptions, feelings, and thoughts as they relate to our potential to prey upon either.

When we take a look at the continuum of dark psychology, it is often going to be based on the range of inhumanity that is used. Think of it this way. Jeffrey Dahmer and Ted Bundy were both horrible serial killers. But Dahmer was doing these acts because he was looking for companionship and Bundy did it to inflict pain just because he was evil. Both would be higher on the dark continuum, but one had a purpose with theirs, and the other did not.

When we look at dark psychology, we are going to see that all people will have some potential when it comes to violence. This potential is going to be found in all of us, and it is going to depend on our backgrounds and our moral compass that will depend on how much we will use this.

If we were able to have a better understanding of the underlying triggers and causes of dark psychology we would have a chance to recognize and even diagnose and then reduce the dangers that are found with its influence.

Dark psychology is something that we can all learn from and benefit from. We just need to take some time to understand it a bit more. It is found inside all of us in some form or another, but most of us are willing to follow the laws and the moral codes in our world and will follow these to not use this latent personality trait. Then there are others who are going to fall onto the continuum and who will find that it is easier for them to use dark psychology in order to get the results and benefits that they are looking for.

Dark Psychology is all around us and is at work every second of every day – you might just not recognize it yet. Schools and universities all over the world have programs dedicated to "psychology" or the study of mind and behavior. Dark Psychology can be thought of as the study of how to manipulate the mind and an individual's behavior by using scientific knowledge already available to us.

Dark Psychology is the shadow of Psychology as we know it today. It's psychology's dark side, it's underbelly, the id to the ego. *While many people go to school to study psychology, the study of the human mind, there isn't necessarily a place to study dark psychology.* Not only because it's we're just becoming to understand it – no.

Those who study dark Psychology hope to know about the human condition – the human brain and humankind's ability to prey upon others' minds and manipulate them for their own purposes. Why would someone want to do this? The reasoning dates back to the evolution of early humankind. The motivation stems from purposeless criminal, aberrant and divergent developments within the human brain. Personality disorders, schizophrenia, manic depressive disorder, and grandiose delusions can all contribute to an individual's abuse of dark psychology, though technically everyone has this potential to victimize other humans and living creatures. While most restrain or sublimate this tendency, some decide to act upon these impulses and use them to manipulate their fellow humans.

While in the development of human beings through the ages, human Psychology has created a sort of "pack mentality" in which survival is based on teamwork and cooperation, dark psychology seeks to understand individuals who tend to do the opposite. Those who display traits of dark Psychology have brain wiring systems that lead to predatory behavior that runs counter to traditional ways of thinking about human behavior.

Using the tools available to you with Dark Psychology can be positive or negative. Much of society see mind control, brainwashing, dark seduction, emotional manipulation as abusive and devious.

But the meaning is in the mind of the beholder.

Much of Dark Psychology rational, and if used properly, can elicit positive outcomes without harm. However, it is valuable to know to understand the history and roots of dark Psychology and its uses, not only so you may be able to use it for good, but also that you might be able to protect yourself from those who might look to use you as part of their ulterior motives.

So who is most likely to use dark tactics? Ultimately, it's those you might have recognized on the school playground getting bullied. Those who, at one time or another, felt "inferior."

Tactics of Dark Psychology

The most commonly used tactics of dark Psychology seen and used are hypnosis, brainwashing, manipulation, seduction, and deception, which all might be referred to the layperson as "mind control." Since humans have been able to communicate, the idea of mind control has been tempting and its secrets have attracted scientists and religious zealots alike. Movies, books, songs, and folktales all perpetuate the allure of being able to control another human being's actions and thoughts with only the power of thoughts and words. Mind control is also at the root of many horror novels and conspiracy theories. It's a dream and a nightmare, both.

Carl Jung and the "Shadow"

Carl Jung was a famous Swiss psychiatrist and psychoanalyst who was a contemporary of Sigmund Freud. Both practiced during the late 1800s and early 1900s when the world was just really beginning to understand what the human brain was capable of. Besides creating the concept of analytical psychology, Jung also discovered and put a name to some of our best known psychological terms including the collective unconscious and the extravert/introvert spectrum. Jung is hands down one of the most influential psychoanalysts of the past two centuries and his idea of the "shadow," also known as the "id" or "shadow aspect/archetype" the part of our consciousness which is the exact opposite of our "ego" or conscious self. This is the side of our brains that many people left unknown, unexplored and untouched.

Over time, Jung's "shadow" or the "id" has earned many nicknames from among different groups including "alter ego" or "repressed self" or even "the dark side." This "shadow" is the same wellspring of energy that powers dark psychology. If someone's shadow is strong, according to Jung, it may make itself visible in dreams as "a person of the same sex as that of the dreamer." Jung believed that the power of the shadow could be released once an individual had an "encounter" with it, in a process referred to as "individuation." But that process is dangerous because once begun, it's very hard to reverse. The more you interact with your shadow, your inner darkness, the more darkness becomes part of your ego and your visible consciousness.

Making the Shadow Conscious

Humans are the end result of evolution and with evolution came out shadow. Humans contain multitudes. Within our brains we have deep, ancient drives for sexual intercourse, self-defense, and even cruelty. We try to keep these hidden and locked up in the present day because as society has evolved, more pressure has been placed on the individual to keep their "animal side" under control.

Other parts of the shadow, which may be harnessed for dark psychological purposes, are actually because of the way we were raised. It's the old "nature versus nurture" argument. Many individuals can remember the time they spoke out in class and were punished by a teacher, or when they did the opposite of their parent's bidding and received a spanking or was grounded.

Many authority figures act this way in response to "unruly" behavior in children because it scares them and makes them feel anxious. Their gut response is to punish, and then criticize, to make sure that they personally never have to deal with feeling uncomfortable again. Of course, in children, the most common defense mechanism to an adult response like this is repression. Repressed children build mental fences, learn how to compartmentalize and not display their true emotion. The more repressed an individual is, the more time and energy their unconscious shadow has to develop.

Think of the mind's shadow as a diamond. The more heat and pressure it receives, and the further and longer it stays underground, the bigger and more brilliant it becomes.

The more repressed the individual, the more likely the shadow is to stay unconscious. That shadow can develop into a proclivity for the use of dark psychology. Some individuals feel magnetism towards the techniques and advantages of dark psychology, those that give them power over other human beings, without being able to explain why. Those with repressed childhood cannot simply forget. They've actually developed a shadow that's capable of thought, desire, and decision making independently of the rest of their conscious.

Simply put, the shadow or the idea can take control. Our ego simply rolls over like a trained dog and lets the id do the talking and the acting. The shadow takes over the individual's emotions and decision-making. So when that individual turns to dark Psychology to manipulate others in their life, little do they realize that they are actually being controlled themselves, by their own shadow.

Not all of those that practice dark psychology are recipients of childhood trauma or have a powerful shadow – though many of them do. And not all victims of childhood trauma become users of dark psychology. Some develop serious mental disorders, alcoholism or drug habits or even develop social anxiety.

If you recognize some of these "shadow-possessed" traits in yourself, it's not time to worry yet. There are ways to avoid this. First, you must accept both your conscious and your subconscious. Our shadow qualities may be unsavory and hard to deal with – they might even be embarrassing or hard to cope with. But every individual has a part of themselves they struggle to accept.

Regardless of what dark secrets lie in your subconscious, it's time to welcome them as part of your whole self. Give them a big hug and a space in your life. These shadow qualities are part of your human experience, and pretending they don't exist will simply give them more control over you. In the end, you need your shadow qualities to feel like they are an important part of your being. It may sound intimidating, but the first step of understanding dark Psychology and how it is used it to become one with your shadow.

Embrace both the light and dark parts of yourself. There are parts of your psyche that are both good and evil.

Make them one. Invite your shadow into your consciousness.

Who Uses Dark Psychology?

Anyone out there who has an understanding of the human mind and its shadow can use dark psychology, but there are personality traits out there that make it more likely for an individual to use dark Psychology for a malevolent goal. These individuals have little regard for the feeling of well-being of others and are hyper-rational. By rational, this means that their own self-interest and success come before everyone and anything else.

These people tend to use covert emotional manipulation, or CEM, to achieve their ends. Mind games, brainwashing, gaslighting and hypnotism are some of their favorites.

These may or may not be the same individuals who use dark seduction to get what they want, including sex. Dark seducers, in particular, are interested in reeling in their victims using sex and sexuality – and they're probably the most skilled at not letting their true intentions become revealed. Dark seducers tend to use proven psychological techniques like mimicry, nonverbal body language and neurolinguistic programming (NLP) to get what they want.

Dark Psychology also appears in cults, both religious and non-religious. Mass marketing and media, national sports leagues and even governments put it to use, maybe even inadvertently. This is possible. Some individuals and groups are so skilled at manipulation and getting what they want, that they've already dipped their toe into dark psychology. But this is not common.

Internet Trolls

Although dark psychology has been around for centuries, the invention of the internet and its proliferation throughout the world has opened up a new realm of possibility for its usage. It turns out that some individuals, who might not have had the ability to use dark psychology in person, due to social awkwardness or some other reason, can use the internet to target and manipulate their victims just the same. In the realm of the internet, we usually just call these individuals "trolls."

There are the annoying internet trolls that just seem to get pleasure out of leaving miserable and idiotic comments on YouTube videos and news articles online. But then there are the trolls that use dating websites, chat forums and other means of online communication to get closer to their victim.

Internet trolls possess massive amounts of patience (like many users of dark Psychology out there) and will lure in people through the art of conversation. It's a combination of CEM, seduction, and NLP that requires a way with words, and once more, a disregard for others' feelings besides their own.

Dark Psychology through the internet is possible in part because of how much information is available to be culled about an intended victim. Social media provides a fertile ground to start. But some internet trolls won't stop there and are actually skilled computer programmers. They'll have no qualms about using their hacking prowess to dig up a victim's background and use it for nefarious purposes in the future.

Internet trolls can also take other forms and names, like cyberstalkers, cyber bullies and online sexual predators. They can be narcissists, Machiavellians, psychopaths, seducers, blackmailers, cult leaders, and emotional manipulators. Their purposes can range from self-aggrandizement to drawing you into a cult. Essentially, most of the dark Psychology can now take place on the internet, which is something to remember as you innocently browse through Facebook or Twitter, Reddit, or your online dating account.

Users of dark Psychology are also likely to have an inferiority complex. Though not all of them do, it is a common trait correlated especially with individuals that use techniques of dark seduction, emotional manipulation, and brainwashing. The inferiority complex usually manifests itself during childhood, when the individual might have undergone some sort of trauma. Possible examples include having been physically smaller than school mates or possessing social awkwardness. The manipulator could have also had a childhood where they felt as if they weren't intelligent enough or "perfect" enough. Often times this is coupled with childhood emotional and physical abuse, either at the hands of a relative or close family friend.

As a result, the child grows up to be an adult that never wants to feel like that again. That child wants to be a big grown up, invincible, incapable of being hurt and completely capable of inflicting their will on others, whatever it may be. Studies of dark Psychology users also show that they have a proclivity towards perfection. Though many average humans are intellectually aware that true perfection is unattainable and a fantasy, users of dark psychology tend to believe that manipulation will help them at least rise above their peers and get them closer to perfection than if they were to never use dark psychology.

Moving Forward

So essentially, anyone can use dark Psychology if they want to. Even you, reader, can become a user of dark psychology, given the information and tools within this book. Think about why you picked this book to read. Chances are that there are others like you who are reading for the same reason. Keep that in mind.

Getting the hang of understanding dark Psychology can be a bit hard at times. Like all of the inventions of humankind, like space travel, harnessing electricity and the wheel it came from a long and lengthy process of trial and error. That's essentially what dark Psychology. It takes practice to understand, wield, and resist. But that's no reason to get discouraged. Just by picking this book to read, you've shown that you're ready to learn. That's the first step.

Dark Psychology can feel magical and it can be intoxicating, as any kind of power is. Just like how some of the world's richest people get drunk on power and abuse it, users of dark Psychology can become enamored with the power that is eventually revealed to them. This is a warning to keep yourself in check if you prepare to mimic any of the techniques in this book.

A good way to stay balanced while practicing dark Psychology is keeping a log. This can be handwritten or on your computer, but make sure that it's private, so you feel comfortable writing whatever thoughts and feelings come to your mind. Record that day's feelings, what techniques you tried, and the results. Keep looking back on this to see how you've progressed. The "feelings" part is especially essential for maintaining your consciousness and making sure you don't lose your self. Reread your entries every time you write a new one. It's important to keep reminding yourself who you are because of dark Psychology is a deep, powerful force that can sweep you away like a riptide.

Back to the Shadow

Before drawing this chapter to a close, let's return to the idea of Carl Jung's shadow once more. It's one of the keystones of dark psychology. After you've finished this book and if you're interested in further reading, pick up Jung's "Psychology of the Unconscious," published in 1912, "The Archetypes and the Collective

Unconscious," published in 1934, or "Psychology and Alchemy," published in 1944.

It's hard to say if Carl Jung were around today if he would approve of how dark psychology has progressed. But he would surely be impressed.

So the shadow is just part of who we are as human beings. Well, most people are not willing to accept that, and in fact, will do anything to block out this part of their psyche. Most people don't want to acknowledge that they have "bad parts" of their personality or brain, and they would like to keep it concealed. Societal pressure tells us to do this.

The best method of keeping our shadow locked up, never to see the light of day? The individual becomes malicious anyway – criticizing and judging and rebuking other people that don't live up to our "ideal" version of a virtuous human being. Despite the fact that locking up the shadow is a form of self-loathing, many people paradoxically live as if their moral standards and way of living were superior to anyone else's.

Which would you rather be? The person who lies to themselves about the reality of human consciousness, or the person who takes the good with the bad, and the dark with the light?

Secret Powers

No, embracing your shadow and diving into dark Psychology isn't going to give you the power of invisibility or flight or super strength. But there are a lot of benefits to embracing the darker parts of our consciousness. The shadow possesses some of our deepest creative powers.

Once you break free from society's expectations about how you "should behave" your repressed abilities can come to the fore. Think of a punished individual with a strong shadow as a plant. That plant needs water and sunshine. It will shrivel and die if locked up in a closet for too long.

The best example of repressed shadows and emerging dark Psychologyusers are individuals who question authority and are "against the man." They dress differently, think differently, vote differently, speak differently. They're just, well, different.

While some might think of this anti-social, self-reliant behavior as problematic or dangerous or defiant of authority, this "lone wolf" syndrome is a way to identify dark Psychologyusers. They'll develop eventually, but unfortunately, societal pressure to behave often traps young and gifted individuals into its the web of expectation. Their intellectual growth is stunted and trapped. When finally released, as a person with a strong shadow and proclivity toward dark Psychology always will be, the individual that was stunted and threatened becomes a threat to those around them.

If only we learned how to accept and encourage our children for who they are, instead of diagnosing them with problematic psychological conditions and then dismissing them. The potential that has been wasted has been enormous. But that stops here, and with you, dear reader.

If you have the opportunity to either have a child or mentor a child who seems to be struggling to integrate their shadow, encourage them. There's no place in this world for shame or belittlement, especially from adults to children. It may seem a bit odd and unnatural at first, but you're doing the world a favor by letting this young individual explore who they are naturally. Don't let their mind become a waste.

You, dear reader, are lucky. You have a second chance. It's likely that when you were a child you had tendencies towards dark psychology and embracing your shadow, and maybe it scared your parents or your teachers a bit. They punished you and tried to put you in a box. Not anymore.

There isn't one specific way to welcome the shadow back into our lives and consciousness: The methods vary from person to person. The best tip is to become comfortable with feeling uncomfortable. Think of what you have to gain: solidarity with your own mind, a sense of self, and true power if wielded and practiced correctly. There's no reason to not welcome the darker parts of your psyche into your life. If you do, a whole new world of understanding human interaction is open to you.

Chapter 2 - Aspects of Dark Psychology

Dark psychology has many different aspects and elements that encompass it. While it is true that we all have these elements within us to some degree, we are not all prone to using them all the time. Most of us will use them when we feel there is no other course for us to take, so we get manipulative.

Ordinary people prefer not to deceive or manipulate. They will usually lean towards doing things in a more honest way and try their best not to hurt those around them. They will eventually go dark if they feel they were pushed into using these techniques. However, not everyone operates like this.

There are people who, for various reasons that aren't always obvious, will dive straight into these tactics as their go-to. They can be for our own good at times, but they often aren't. They will use these tricks on unsuspecting people regardless of the effects they might have on them.

These are usually people who are damaged and live their lives expressing their inner demons in toxic ways.

However, there are those who will use dark psychology because they are what can be considered cold-hearted or even evil. They usually have no regard for the wellbeing of other people whatsoever.

This chapter will give you some insight into how these people may behave. What are some of the most common tactics you will find people using on you in contexts that may have nothing to do with your work? Some of them might be used on you in your social life. The hope is that deeper insight into these tools that have probably been used against most people, will allow them to know what to look out for and perhaps react accordingly. The other hope is that it may help people use them to change their lives for the better in various aspects of their lives be it in their careers, their education, their social lives, or even their love lives.

Psychology Demystified

There are varied definitions of emotions plus some existing literature attempts to compare emotions with feelings in a bid to justify which of both precedes the other. Taking all information and viewpoints into consideration, we can define emotions on three different levels.

Physically: Feelings are reactions from the brain's subcortical sections in response to stimuli. These reactions generate biochemical responses within your body thus changing one's physical condition. They can in turn compel one to action on any matter that stirs the emotions in the threatening or enjoyable way. For this reason, they are seen as part of human survival instincts also.

Mentally: Emotions are normal responses that provide rise to certain thoughts and circumstances of the mind, changing one's state of mind with regards to the stimuli. For this reason, our thoughts are influenced by emotions before we can even think them often! It also dates back to remembering how someone or matter made you feel as the emotional memory space is stored for you to mentally think about down the road.

Emotionally: This seems like an obvious one however the emotional component of emotions is usually oddly the hardest part for most people to grasp! It exists within us beyond the physical and mental elements somewhere. This is the primary of emotion itself; what we feel, how we experience, and the role these feelings play inside our lives. Simply, it is the overall emotional condition of being.

Feelings create an endless response cycle between your physical body and brain for better or worse. They can control your activities or help enhance them - this all depends on your personal relationship with them and your emotional state to be. Overall, feelings are responses to different circumstances that go far beyond the physical features of chemicals releasing within the body.

Emotional senses range between cheerfulness, shock, and anxiety, to sorrow, hatred, and rage. Although feelings are an important part of human living, they may affect your personal conduct and sometimes, you can risk attaching feelings to everything.

Although these skills are essential for the workplace, they will help you improve your relationships outside of work also. To build up, and perfect, your emotional intelligence you need to start paying even more attention to emotions, yours' and others', start to pay attention more and talk less, and make an effort to become more available to other people's viewpoint.

So what exactly is Dark Psychology?

Dark Psychology refers to your developed capacity to identify, appreciate, control, and use emotions to advantage yourself as well as others confidently. This definition could be split into four basic categories: Recognition: To become alert to your own emotions also to recognize your relationship with them.

Appreciation: This can be the most difficult aspect to master since you must figure out how to appreciate your emotions for what they are. Only one time you accept them and find a genuine appreciation for them is it possible to move on to control them in a healthy manner.

Control: Many people confuse this factor with suppression of emotion. To suppress them is indeed a kind of control nonetheless it is forced and only short-term. Suppression leaves you more hurt and susceptible to eruption over time. The purpose here is to allow emotions to release in a controlled way so that they look for a healthy release beneficial to you as well as your interactions.

Confidence: The final aspect of EQ where you can effectively use your emotions in conversation to relieve tension, pull through challenging conditions, resolve squabbles & dissensions, and be empathetic to others. Consequently, a strongly developed sense of emotional intelligence can help you establish and comprehend momentous and emotional episodes in the lives of those around you. At the smallest amount, emotional cleverness equips you having the ability to know your emotions, this is of these feelings, and the potential results your emotions have on those around you. The theory concept here is based on understanding and managing your emotions.

It is important to realize that emotional intelligence is a learned skill and not necessarily a birthright. To gain this skill, you have to train yourself. The good news is that you can sufficiently learn it anytime in your life, which is also why there is no need a good reason to lack this essential skill!

Although most people generally know what emotions are, it is important to first define and understand exactly what is being referred to throughout this written publication.

Have you ever pondered on the inner workings of the minds of certain heinous criminals or those everyday people who display some deviant characters? You may have asked yourself what they feel, think, or the motivation behind their actions. Do they feel pity or regret? This part of our psyche is not so separate from our beliefs, faith, goals, ideologies, and culture. In fact, some of the most criminal and horrid behaviors have often originated from them. But dark psychology makes the point that these actions may not, and quite often do not, have any particular goal.

Usually, when an individual goes out of their way to victimize or manipulate someone else, the drive behind such actions is money, vengeance, sex, love, or power.

This type of behavior can be easily understood, as most of us can relate to such emotions. But there are those whose motivation does not come from any of those driving factors. They hurt, kill, and manipulate people just because. This inherent darkness or evil, as some would term such actions, is present in the psyche of every human being, whether in times past or in our modern society. There are no exceptions. This nature, latent or manifested to cause harm to those who have done us no wrong, is a very complex study indeed, but one which must be undertaken for the purpose of the continuous flourishing of society.

If left unchecked, the growing population of iPredators, arsonists, serial killers, thieves, and other forms of violent and harmful behaviors would become too much of a problem to then be controlled.

Many would object at the generalization that contained in them are such propensities for purposeless evil. Yet, even those fleeting dark thoughts would say otherwise. For many of us, these grotesque images and thoughts of ways to undo another person for no particular reason do not stay in our minds very long, and we cringe when they cross our conscious thoughts or when we act, however briefly, in their direction. But, whether full-blown or short-lived, these thoughts and actions are proof that we all are capable of some degree of 'evil.' Within the study of dark psychology, some terms arise which should be understood. They include dark singularity, dark continuum, and dark factor. Dark singularity is used to illustrate the severity of evil acted out by those who fall within this category of dark psychology. Like singularity in physics which refers to the center of a black hole; the densest phenomena in space which has been discovered. Individuals categorized in dark singularity exhibit traits which can only be described as absolutely deviant and extremely cruel. Dark continuum is an imagined area wherein lies people of varying severity of dark psychology. From the least criminal to the most violent make up the population in dark continuum. In mathematical terms, dark singularity can be seen as a subset of a dark continuum, as it can found within the latter. Dark continuum ranges from those individuals who have evident motivation for the acts of evil they commit, and those who do the same for no reason at all. On the most severe part of a dark continuum (in terms of how grievous the action was, and the thought which birthed it) lies dark singularity. To the right of the dark continuum are the actions resulting from dark psychology, while to the left is the psychology behind it. Dark factor is that part in the psyche of everyone in which rests the potential for evil. Included in the dark factor are also those experiences which makes more or less likely that an individual might engage in deviant behaviors or acts of evil.

Introduction to the infamous dark triad

The dark triad may sound like something out of a Hollywood movie, but it is actually the cornerstone of dark psychology and, by extension, this book. The dark triad refers to the three personality types that inspired the inception of dark psychology. In fact, these three personality types are where the techniques found in dark psychology stems from. What are these big three that are the basis for a field of study that may seem so bizarre then?

The three personality types that make up the dark triad, while seemingly self-explanatory, can be difficult to spot because of some unfortunate misunderstandings about their nature and origin. The dark triad consists of: Machiavellianism, Narcissism and Psychopathy. While these may seem to paint pictures that give them away off the bat, it is often not quite that simple.

People associate Machiavellianism with a political type who took 'The Prince' a little too seriously; Narcissism as someone who is enamored with their own image; and a Psychopath as someone straight out of a slasher film. The real-life examples of these traits are more sinister than that as they can easily slip under the radar and operate under the veil of the general public's ignorance.

The dark triad is associated with personality traits that show a strong link to Borderline Personality Disorder (BPD). Most people may find that they manifest at least some of the qualities represented on the dark triad, but people who have very high concentrations of one part of the triad or even some combination of the three can be terribly destructive forces in any given aspect of everyday life.

Chapter 3 - Victims Of Dark Psychology

Dark tactics can happen to anyone at any time. There are different categories of people who are targeting those who practice dark psychology. Many psychopaths will target specific victims because they know that they are vulnerable. They know who they are looking for, and when they find the right victims, they have their way with them. Not everyone is a target, but it is good to know if you could be one in the future.

Those who are looking for potential victims will prey on those who have to please everyone they meet. Many call this the "disease to please." Psychopaths can spot this trait out of a crowd. The minute they meet people like this, they know exactly what to do! These people are very polite and kind, no matter what type of feelings they get from people. This is the perfect person for anyone who uses dark tactics to prey upon.

Another group of people they prey on are those who are very vulnerable. Generally, women who have suffered a divorce, a death, or a breakup will be the first ones on their radar. This vulnerability leaves them wide open for psychopaths to take advantage of them. They are also seeking approval of someone, especially if they just suffered a tragic break up. This is when the psychopaths slide right in and try to take the place of the person who left them. They show the victim that they approve of them, and they will shower them with kind words and compliments. Some will even shower them in gifts and money to get what they want from them.

Victims also fall into the categories of having low self-worth and esteem, the inability to say no to people, a very cloudy sense of their own identity, and low self-reliance. Sometimes they are naïve and young. Immaturity is seen in a lot of the child and teenage victims of predators. These younger victims also have some emotional dependency on those who are older and wiser than them.

There are other traits that potential victims have that may seem like part of the predator's personality. One of these is greed. Many victims have some dark tendencies, and greed is one that they use a lot. When a predator finds a victim, sometimes the victims stay with the predator because of what they can get from them. This is what causes a lot of victims to stay in a relationship longer and hold to see what they can get from them. This is when we will see harm or even death come to that victim.

Victims of predators are often lonely and looking for a way to change how they feel. They want someone to be with and love them back. The loneliness factor is another reason that people will stay with predators for so long. Some victims are also masochistic when it comes to being preyed upon. Masochists enjoy feeling pain. They get pleasure when predators treat them with harmful actions and words.

There is no doubt that anyone can fall victim to a predator. It is important to watch out if you are ever feeling vulnerable or lonely. The best thing to do is to call a trusted friend, neighbor, or relative when you are feeling this way. You don't want to end up as part of someone's dark tactics.

Chapter 4 - Dark Psychology And You

Now that you have learned all the significant details of the practice of dark psychology, you have enough information for a strictly useful, not just informational, chapter. What this means is, now that you have received so much information about how dark psychology functions and how it might be used with enough practice and skill, you are ready for a chapter made specifically for you where you are now in your learning process, whether you already feel confident in your dark abilities or you are still relatively unsure of yourself. If you are unsure of yourself, in fact, this chapter should give you the confidence needed to work through the ideas and exercises in the rest of the book again so that you will, ultimately, be on your way to a comprehensive mastery of dark psychology.

That fact is, quite simply, that being dark, amoral, and self-interested in all of your pursuits, being fully of the dark psychology mindset and worldview, in other words, not only does not necessarily but should not preclude you being an easygoing and well-liked person. It should is emphasized above because it is actually very useful, as a practitioner of dark psychology, to avoid the attention that the overtly conniving and the socially untalented face. If you get too much attention of the wrong kind, people will realize the ways that you are thinking and the things you are endeavoring to do, and, because most people are not as enlightened as dark psychology practitioners when it comes to things like morality, truth, and empathy, they will not look kindly on you if they discover you for who you are.

You do not have to worry too much about this, though, even if you are, personally, not the best at being likable, because the methods of dark psychology can make anyone likable. That's right, despite their inherently sinister and dark nature, dark psychology applied correctly can make you super-likable, and that's exactly what this chapter will show you.

10 Ways to Become a Super-Likable Person using Dark Psychology

What exactly does dark psychology have to do with being likable, though? In one sense of the term, dark psychology has a lot more to do with being hated than being liked. People, by and large, do not like dark things, especially things that can easily affect them negatively if they come in too close a contact with them. In another sense, however, dark psychology is a more straightforward path to being liked, or even loved, than traditional, moral, and empathic based lifestyles. This is because with dark psychology, if being liked is your goal, then nothing needs to stand in the way of achieving it. This kind of thinking stands in marked relief from the normal way of going about life, in which one has goals but only follows them when ethics, morals, and emotions allow one to do so. You will see from the following set of instructions how incredibly useful dark psychology can be for the aspiring socialite or climber. If you follow these ideas closely, all your dreams of social prominence will come true!

You can use dark psychology to become the life of the party, for starters. Have you ever languished in the corner of a crowded party for hours, struggling in vain to work up the courage to talk to strangers, worried that you might put your foot in your mouth, stutter, or have nothing to say? Many if not most people share in this experience at least once or twice in their lives. It is not spoken about often, and generally not covered at length when it is spoken about, but it is, nonetheless, a very common human experience. Most likely, it will continue to be just that, because people, as a group, struggle to change all that much. You, however, as an individual, can absolutely change, and you can change in a way that takes into account the fact that everyone else will stay the same. What does this mean? It means that you can harness your past awkwardness as another bit of information to be analyzed and understood using a dark psychology perspective. If you already know that most people feel somewhat awkward at parties, what do you do? You project what you know they want back onto them, and you determine what they want because you yourself have wanted it in the past. Think about it, have you not wanted a charismatic person to initiate a conversation with you at a party before? Don't you appreciate it when that happens? Well, forget about your own insecurities and become that person for other people! This is a scenario where "Fake it till you make it" is actually incredibly apt advice. The more you become what others want, which is the charismatic, boisterous partygoer, the more people will flock to you, thereby giving you the confidence to take it even further. Don't be afraid to bully people into having fun to a certain degree. The real win here comes from building a number of followers at the party, such that any new person who walks in sees that you are the center of attention. If you follow this concept for long enough, you truly will become the life of the party, and it will be because you were smart enough to use dark psychology and push aside your foolish insecurities in order to win.

You can stand out at work using dark psychology. This one was actually covered in passing in the first half of the book. It actually makes quite a bit of straightforward sense if you have been able to follow everything in the book so far. Basically, dark psychology requires in almost all situations that its practitioners focus and spend a large or at least a sizable amount of time studying and coming to understand their subjects. Well, this skill is almost always useful in an office or work setting, provided you have coworkers, and you do not give them attention in a socially incorrect or uncomfortable way. What it comes down to is splitting your focus and attention between the tasks that make up the job you are paid to do and the tasks that makeup is interrelating with the people with whom you work. If you pay them the right kind of attention, and the right amount, not only will you get the positive byproduct of having more friends at the office, if that is something you want, but, more importantly, you will have collected enough information on these coworkers of yours to start to manipulate or influence social situations to your own benefit. Perhaps you realize that one of your "friends" a couple of cubicles over is a massive geek for Marvel movies. What do you do? You start up a couple of conversations with him about his favorite topic. You mention how super excited you are for the next installation of whatever movie is coming out next. Then, you go down the hall, and you talk about cooking shows, or Patti Smith's music, or whatever it is that the person who works down the hall likes to do on his or her off time. You get a general idea. The important thing is to find common ground with as many people as possible, such that everyone or almost everyone likes you. Then, your boss, and quite possibly your boss's boss, will start to notice you as an outlier. That is, they will start to notice you as an outlier in the most positive sense of the word. This process may take some time, but you can rest assured it will end in your benefit very squarely.

You can use dark psychology to project confidence wherever you need more confidence in your life. This one goes back to the first way to become a super-likable person, the one in which the best way to become the life of the party by way of dark psychology methodology was faking confidence and exuberance until those behaviors became natural by virtue of the fact that you had attracted the attention necessary from other people actually to have those behaviors. The scenario may be different, but the central principle is the same. In this case, in which you may not be in a situation that calls for drawing attention to yourself, your first objective should be analyzing whatever situation you want to master to figure out what it is that you need in that situation to maximize your own confidence. Maximizing confidence, despite what many normal people might tell you about internal worth, is all about your status relative to the other people involved in the situation. If you are alone and still feel a lack of confidence, ask yourself why, and then ask yourself if there are any people on whom you feel fixated or to whom you feel inferior. Then, ask yourself how you can reframe your relationship with those people to reorient the power dynamic to your benefit. This is the arithmetic you must use in place of normal human decision making based around morality. If the situation involves other people directly, the same question applies: why is it that your relationship with those people is such that you feel unconfident? This is the only question you should ask yourself, and the answer should be built around data that is changeable by way of action and not introspection. Self-knowledge is key to many, many tools in the dark psychology toolbox, but it is not the solution in most cases. It is something that aids in finding a solution, which should always be rooted in interpersonal action. If you find yourself unable to find confidence no matter what you do to improve your standing in the social hierarchy of a given situation, what you actually need is a therapy of some kind or another, most likely Lacanian analysis. The Lacanian analysis allows for introspection without the indoctrination of most forms of psychotherapy, wherein you will be required to accept certain false premises about the importance of having a firm, or even an unbreakable sense of self. This kind of thinking will not assist you in becoming the Father – to use a Lacanian term – of all those over whom you wish to be in a given social hierarchy.

You can make sure you do not put up with people you do not like every again through dark psychology. This one has a lot to do with the vision of hierarchy and confidence that was spelled out in the last one. That is to say, not having to put up with people you do not like has a lot to do with having the social station necessary to reject interactions you would rather not have. Think about it; if you are emotionally or socially not at the top of the hierarchy in a given social situation, say the hierarchy at your place of employment, it doesn't matter what official role you play. You could be the supervisor of five employees or even the boss in charge of the whole business, but if you have not established dominance or your place at the top of the pecking order, then you can still theoretically be beholden to others around you and forced to engage with them despite the fact that you do not like them. Of course, gaining the upper hand hierarchically while you are the boss is much easier than gaining it while you are not, to continue the workplace example. You can always fire someone to establish dominance over the rest, or fire someone because you plainly do not like them, thereby arriving at the desired situation anyway. Say you are not the boss, though, or say that you are not at work. What do you do? You have to apply methods of dark psychology directly, most likely methods of manipulation will do. You may be wondering, "How will this make me a super-likable person? People like this are absolutely insufferable." The answer is that this is only a cultural perception. People like confidence quite a bit because it makes them feel safe, and with enough confidence, charisma, that natural draw of positive attention and likability, flows like water from a waterfall into your effect and posture. So, no, maximizing status and confidence will not and does not negatively affect others' opinions of you.

You can make as much money as you want to make with dark psychology, all the time! This one is less a question of confidence and more a question of minimizing normal human morality in the way you organize and run your life. Recall, again, the example of the older, lonely person in the coffee shop and how a dark psychology practitioner would deal with him or her compared to a normal person, even a normal person who was less moral yet still not amoral in his or her dealings. The way that hypothetical went, wherein the dark psychology practitioner Person 3 managed to gain indefinite thousands from his or her work manipulating this older lonely poor person, shows you how significant the full dark psychology worldview is to your success in dark psychology, especially when it comes to finances. Person 2, who existed as a stand-in for the not overly empathetic or moral but still normal, pragmatic worldview, only managed to get the price of a meal out of the older person. To zero in on self-interest and the fact that other people's emotional and subconscious lives are also aspects of self-interest is key, here. Recognize that all situations are potential opportunities to make money off of others, that all people with enough attention paid and analyses made are susceptible to your influence. Whether you enact that influence through manipulation, dark persuasion, mind control, or some other dark psychology derived technique is no matter. The important thing is that, if you want the money trees of the world to bloom for you, you have to know how to look for them, and you can only see them in the first place if you tap into the dark psychology mindset and start seeing other people as means to ends, methods for succeeding in your own life, tools. Again, the endlessly reiterated point returns, but this time with a slight addition. Dark psychology is a set of tools, but it is a set of tools that means to, in part, turn everything else into tools, too. Without truth or morally, emotionally-motivated mindsets to organize your mind, in other words, you should start to view all other people and things as things that can, if necessary, be manipulated, as tools. Completing the process of taking on this dark psychology mindset will undoubtedly turn to gain money into a simple, simple task. Improve your job whenever you want by being exactly the kind of person your new employer needs, or at least projecting the image of the exact kind of person your new employer needs. Or, manipulate and darkly persuade your way through life. The important thing is, with correct and intense enough application, you will never want for money again. And this, again, is a likable trait. Everyone loves someone who can pay his or her own way, no matter the circumstance, and a fast track to alienating people and losing friends is broke. You can charm your way into any event with dark psychology. Maybe you want to be the life of the party what, first, you have to get into the party! It may sound somewhat cartoonish, or like a movie, but you, too, can schmooze and sneak your way into social events or situations without having been invited if you are shrewd enough dark psychology practitioner. This one comes down to identifying the needs and weaknesses of the few people who have the power to get you in. If you have some time to pre-plan, if the event is at least a couple days off, in other words, this process is as simple as figuring out who is running the party and deploying a short term manipulation strategy against them. Ask yourself, in that case, what that person seems to want. What does he or she seem insecure about, or what does he or she lack emotionally? Once you have that answer, you can figure out how to provide that thing, or at least the impression of that thing, for him or her. Alternately, you could play on his or her sense of empathy by expressing some kind of negative emotion at them. This would work by claiming he or she had slighted you emotionally. You do not want the emotional slight to be about the event you want to get into, because this is too transparent. Instead, it should be about something else, or, even better, it should be an exposure of some so-called moral shortcoming that that person has. No matter what, make sure to very subtly guiding the interaction, after the negativity has been deployed, to the party, but wait for that person to invite you. If, on the other hand, you are trying to get into an event that is already in progress, you are going to have to use suggestions. Remember, suggestion can be very powerful, even when used against a stranger in a short amount of time. Make sure, if you attempt this, that you have learned two things well: target selection and conversational suggestion. Make sure your target has direct access to space, and make sure you are capable of deploying suggestions without drawing undue attention to your social interaction. Re-read the section on selection in the chapter on mind control for a refresher if you must. Regardless, if you are persistent, you will get into social events with dark psychology. It is only a matter of time.

You can use dark psychology to take that beautiful object of your desires out whenever you want! This should be clear by now, but thinking in a self-interested and amoral way does not limit or eliminate your human desire. Far from it, it frees desire up and allows it flourish and reign in your life as nature intended In a sense, living by the dark psychology creed is all about being honest in the self-interested pursuit of your own desires. That being said, it is only natural that you will still be physically, romantically, and sexually attracted to particular people, which is to say that you will still see some relationships as ends in themselves. The difference, however, will come in what and how you are willing to turn those desired relationships into actual ones. So, how can you use dark psychology to be super-likable to that person you have had feelings for as long as you can remember? Well, if you have been working to maximize your status in all situations and groups as well as working to maximize your money, then that person may very well already have feelings for you! If not, though, the solution is quite simple. You must zero in on his or her wavelength in order to exploit it. It is basic, and classic, manipulation based on knowledge of his or her psyche. With enough expertise in dark psychology, in general, this should be a walk in the park.

You can get your coworkers' respect and keep it with dark psychology no matter what. This one is in some ways a variation of standing out at work, but it zeroes in more on the concept of understanding that the official pecking order at work is not the same as the subterranean, subconscious one that nonetheless exists in everyone's mind including your own. That is to say, there is a hierarchy that has nothing to do with bosses, assistant managers, clerks, or janitors, and it comes down to the kind of energy you project. Remember the Nietzschean concept of the active and unfettered individual put in opposition to the reactive, controlled individual? No amount of power can make a person into an active and unfettered individual if they are too cowardly and weak, and this includes your boss. So, how do you get everyone's respect? By displaying your assertiveness, of course. In this case, very little individual analysis and attention are actually necessary, because a part of that group or mass psychology that was covered in the chapter on persuasion is at work in any workplace, which is to say that there are certain rules and group mentalities that pretty much all modern workplaces have. So, a certain kind of easy-going assertiveness that contains some kindness but just as much self-defense and brusqueness, as needs are, should turn you into the most respected and high-status member of any office or break room. It is important to highlight the emphasis, here, of the variations between easy-going and assertive. You can not simply maintain a middle level between the two attitudes; both must be present at different times in your day-to-day demeanor. You do not, after all, want to blend into the furniture, nor do you want to come across as bitter or rude. The amount of each necessary will change workplace by workplace, but in the end, you want to find the right amount of both easy-going-ness and assertiveness such that everyone understands you to be a simultaneously calm or "chill" on the one hand and confident or no-nonsense on the other kind of person.

You can have the best kids around with dark psychology. This one is a good litmus test for how committed you actually are to the dark psychology worldview and thinking process. If you understand it for what it is, which is a more honest and productive all-encompassing worldview than the normative one than you will be more than willing to apply its lessons to your relationship with your children. The way this works, rather than manipulating your children, is in bringing them into the fold. So many of the problems of childhood come from a lack of literacy when it comes to other human beings' psyches and the child's inability to control his or her own psyche. If you have children, do you not think it would benefit them to learn from the jump on how to exercise control over themselves and practice analysis of others' subconscious states? It benefits your children directly to think about the world this way, and it benefits you by way of association. If you have children, you will be thought of more positively, and you will be more likable if those children are the best and super-likable themselves. It just makes sense! What is more, it will make your children more likely to excel in life and business, thereby becoming the conniving, amoral apples of their parents' eyes as well as their parents' community's eyes.

In conclusion, you can basically excel at whatever, wherever, whenever with dark psychology. The summation of all these examples of ways to become super-likable through dark psychology is this: dark psychology is an excellent means of not just becoming super-likable, but being exactly who you want to be wherever you happen to be at the time! Of course, the kind of confidence and self-assuredness this brings out in you will, without a doubt, make you super-likable no matter what else you are pursuing, and this is because people respect and highly value those traits. So, start to establish dark psychology tools in your day-to-day life, and you will undoubtedly find that you are attracting positive attention from people wherever you go. In most cases, you will know, coldly and cynically, that liking does not entail all that much more than projection and self-interest, but that is okay provided you are still benefiting from the positive energy being projected at you, from which you will absolutely benefit. It is a kind of feedback loop that, if done correctly, can only

generate positive results.

Chapter 5 - Deception

Once manipulation is identified, the next step is to get through it. Overcoming manipulation can be very challenging. In some cases, a 60 year-old-man might realize just now that his 85 year-old-mother is manipulative. They might never get through their issues, but they should still be confronted. Manipulation takes a part of both the abuser and the victim. It can ruin people's lives, altering the direction they take and affecting the rest of their years. Manipulation can be hard to identify and even harder to overcome.

It can be done, and it should be attempted to get through. In a relationship based around manipulation, there might not be any coming back. Sometimes, people might just have to break up. You might have to get a divorce or stop calling your mom. It takes two people to partake in a manipulative scenario. Not both people will end up identifying it as a manipulative situation, however. In that case, the person that realizes what's actually going on might just have to move on, the manipulator never realizing the damage they caused.

This can be a challenging part of overcoming manipulation. Usually, some instance of codependency formed, making it even harder to break away.

Know Your Worth

The first step in overcoming manipulation is for the victim to identify that they still have value. A manipulator likely took everything from their victim. They belittled them, ridiculed them, and made them feel as though what they thought didn't matter. In some situations, they might have even used gaslighting tactics to make their victims feel as though they're insane. It can be hard for a victim to then recognize just how much value they still have once they become aware of the manipulation.

It's important for everyone to know, no matter who is reading this, that you have worth. Everyone has value. No one deserves to be manipulated. No one deserves to feel as though they don't have any purpose, reason, or value. You have the right to be treated justly, and with respect from other people. You are allowed to express your emotions, feelings, wants, and opinions. No one else has the right to tell you how to feel. You set your own boundaries, and no one else gets to decide for you. If you feel sad about something, that is completely valid. No one gets to decide if what they say hurts you or not. Not everyone might intentionally mean to hurt you, but that doesn't mean you're not allowed to still feel bad. You have the right to feel the way you do, and you have the same right to express those beliefs.

If you feel like you need to protect yourself, you are just in doing so. If you feel like your safety is being threatened, or someone is taking advantage of you, you have the right to remove yourself from that situation without guilt. No one gets to treat you badly, and though that can be hard for many of us to hear, it's the truth.

Manipulators aim to take these thoughts away. They want to deprive their victims of their rights in order to work towards getting what they want. This can't happen anymore. It's up to the manipulator's victims to now recognize their worth and stop the cycle of manipulation.

Don't Be Afraid to Keep Your Distance

Many people that feel as though they're being manipulated end up being too afraid to do anything about it. They have been stripped of their own thoughts and opinions, their own feelings invalidated and instead focus on how other people feel. Those that have been continually manipulated might be afraid to leave those that have hurt them. They've depended on those that abused them for so long they don't know where else to go.

You're allowed to keep your distance. You don't have to feel guilty about protecting yourself. It can be hard to separate yourself from a manipulator, especially in a romantic relationship. You might see the very weaknesses that cause their manipulative behavior. Maybe in a relationship, a boyfriend's dad was an abusive alcoholic, and it greatly hurt him. It also caused his violent manipulative behavior that led him to hitting his girlfriend on a few occasions. It's true that he has his own pain, but that doesn't mean he's allowed to inflict it on others. The girlfriend has every right to leave her boyfriend and find her own peace and protection.

Ask what is really lost by leaving the person that's manipulating you. More often than not, value in a relationship is placed on codependent tendencies. A person is afraid to leave not because they love their manipulator, but because they are afraid to be alone. It can be scary to be on your own, but mostly because manipulators put that idea in their victims in the first place. Manipulators will trick their victims into staying with them because deep down, they know that the victim will be just fine without them.

It's Not Your Job to Change Them

Once manipulation is recognized, the next step is to try to talk to the person about the manipulation. It's time to get down to the root issues of the relationship and figure out what can be done to help both partners get what they need, instead of just the manipulator. There has been an imbalance of power for far too long, and it's time to rebalance.

Unfortunately, not many manipulators are willing to admit their faults and later change their behavior. Instead, they'll do whatever they can to distract others from their faults, placing the blame on their victims instead. When this happens, the victim has to accept that their manipulator isn't going to change, and they must find the strength to leave.

There will likely be a desire to change the other person and help them improve their life as well. Not everyone will always be on the same page of their journey towards self-discovery. It can be hard to accept for some victims, but they have to realize that it's not their job to change their manipulator.

You can only help a person so much, and if they're not willing to change or improve themselves, it's not going to happen. Many people wait around for the other to change in their relationship, hoping their manipulation will get better. If a person isn't aware of their behavior and aren't actively trying to change it, nothing is going to happen in the end.

Hypnosis

If mind control is the best set of manipulation strategies for beginners to pick up and be able to learn quickly, then hypnosis is the next natural step in the process towards becoming a master of manipulation. In general, hypnosis lasts longer and is far more powerful than mind control is, although it also requires more skill to successfully pull off. While hypnosis has some concepts that overlap with mind control and brainwashing, it also has completely unique components, which can make it more challenging to learn. Hypnosis has a long a rich history, and today it is used in a wide variety of fields and industries, including in medicine, sports, psychotherapy, self-improvement, meditation and relaxation, forensics and criminal justice, art and literature, and the military. Of course, all instances of hypnosis share common characteristics no matter what context it is used in, and these same characteristics can come in handy when attempting to manipulate someone else. Having a good understanding of the principles and concepts of hypnosis can turn you from a mediocre manipulator into a highly skilled one.

The Hypnotic Trance

At its core, hypnosis is all about planting ideas into somebody else's subconsciousness in order to influence their consciousness. If you manage to infiltrate a person's subconsciousness with enough skill, they will not be aware of what you are doing, and will never know that you ever influenced them at all. The best way to access someone's subconsciousness is to coax them into a relaxed, meditative state known as a hypnotic trance. Getting your target into a trance is the most difficult part of the process of hypnosis, but once you finally manage to pull it off, you will have a much easier time successfully manipulating them. Putting your target into a trance allows for you to have direct access to their subconsciousness, as their consciousness will no longer be an active part of their mind for the duration of the trance. The trace is what separates hypnosis from mind control, and the ability to induce it in somebody else is what separates a beginner of manipulation from a budding expert.

The best way to think of a hypnotic trance is a form of deep relaxation. You are likely already familiar with the overall concept of the trace, due to portrayals of hypnosis in book, movies, and popular culture in general. Of course, in real life, you cannot put somebody else into a hypnotic trance simply by waving a watch in front of their face or by using a magical code phrase that will put them to sleep. Instead, putting someone into a hypnotic trance takes lots of time and skill, and it may not always work on every single person that you try it out on, especially when you are first starting to attempt to use it. In fact, for the best introduction to the hypnotic trance, you may want to find a friend who is willing to allow you to put them into a trance in order to practice doing it, or if you cannot find someone who is a willing participant, you can always put yourself into a hypnotic trance using this same method. If you fail at putting somebody into a trance, you are likely to face a negative reaction from that person, as they are likely to recognize suspicious behavior when they see it if they still have full awareness of their surroundings. This is why it is important that you practice this technique several times before attempting it on any outsiders, as you are far more likely to succeed in putting somebody into a hypnotic trance if you have some familiarity with how it already works.

The first step in putting your target into a hypnotic trance is to make sure that they are in a sitting position, or even better, lying down. After all, once your target is in the trance and their consciousness has temporarily faded away, they will no longer physically be able to stand up or support the weight of their own body. An action as forceful and abrupt as falling on the floor will be enough to wake them up from the hypnotic trance, and once they have regained their awareness, they will likely want an explanation as to what happened. Obviously, this is not a situation that you want to be caught in, so it is important to make sure that your target's body is in a secure position that will not fall over or cause them to wake up once you have put them in the trance. This also means that you should not attempt to hypnotize anybody unless there is a couch, chairs, a bed, or another piece of comfortable furniture for your target to use. Convincing your target to sit or lay down sounds more difficult than it actually is. Remember that your target will be more likely to sit or lay down if a piece of furniture is offered to them to do so on and that you should be prepared to sit or lay down first, as your target will be more likely to do the same if they are following your lead. If all else fails, you can always mind control them and influence them to sit or lay down where you want them to. Do not worry too much about how you make your target get into the best position and instead focus your attention on what comes after you have already convinced them to do so. The next step in the process of putting someone into a hypnotic trance is to get your target to listen to the sound of your voice. In hypnotic techniques, your voice can be a powerful tool as long as you know how to use it correctly. Take special note of the fact that this step does not instruct you to start a conversation with your target, but rather to get them to listen to you. This is because when attempting to put another person into a hypnotic trance, your voice is not being used to express any meaning or to describe any information, but rather as a way to create a sort of white noise, which will allow your target to slip further and further into a deeply relaxed state. If your target is engaged by what you are saying and tries to respond, then they are not letting go of their awareness, and their consciousness is still very much active. When attempting to put your target in a hypnotic trance, when you are first beginning to speak to them, the content of what you are saying matters a tremendous amount. You need to choose a topic that is interesting enough for them to want to stick around and listen to, but not so interesting that they are completely engrossed in what you are saying and are trying to speak back to you. The topic that you choose is likely to vary from target to target, as everyone has different tastes as to what kind of subject they are willing to pay attention to or not. This is where skills learned under controlling the narrative can come in handy; if you are able to tell a long, meandering story instead of a short and sweet one, especially about something that your target does not particularly care about, then they should begin falling into a hypnotic trance relatively easily. When you are speaking, be sure to use a calm, soothing voice, and choose words and phrases to use that are generally simple and easy to understand. This allows your target to focus on the overall sound of your voice, rather than what exactly you are saying. However, if you make your voice sound too calm and soothing, your target may think that something is wrong with you or may grow suspicious of your intentions. Therefore, try not to sound too much like a guided meditation instructor and instead attempt to model your voice in the style of the narrator of a nature documentary. Keep in mind that your goal is to relax your target, but not to put them to sleep. If you make yourself sound too soothing, you will run the risk of having your target be too relaxed. If your target is asleep, after all, they will not be open to any suggestions that you make, as they will be unconscious. Once you see that your target has fallen into a more and more relaxed state, the content of what you are saying to them will not matter as much, and as long as you keep your voice in a steady, soothing tone, you will not have to worry about what topic you are speaking about any longer.

The Amnesia Technique

The amnesia technique is a verbal test. In it you will ask the potential subject to forget about something for a period of time (it shouldn't be more than a few minutes). For example, you can ask your subject to forget the letter P. Tell them to pretend that the letter P never existed and to forget that you even told them to forget about it. Then ask them to recite the alphabet. People who are moderately or highly suggestible will skip over the letter P (or whatever letter you tell them to forget) and not even realize it. Once again, if the person you tried this test on skips over the letter you told them to forget, they may be a good subject to zone in on.

The Locked Hand Technique

The locked hand technique (also known as the hand clasp technique) is another physical test that the subject will have to be willing to participate in. Like the light/heavy hand technique, it will test just how deeply a person can concentrate on the words you are saying to them and what you are telling them to imagine. Ask your subject to clap their hands together and keep them together, palm to palm. Then tell them to interlace their fingers. Make sure that you maintain fixed eye-contact with them throughout this test and tell them to push their hands together as tightly as they can. Tell them to imagine their hands merging into one piece of solid flesh and bone. After a minute or two, tell them to stop pushing and try pulling their hands apart. Again, a potential manipulation subject will find it hard to pull their hands away from each other.

Chapter 6 - The Power Of Persuasion

The power of persuasion means nothing more than using mental abilities to form words and feelings used to convince other people to do things they may or may not want to do. Some people are better able to persuade than other people. And some people are easier to persuade then other people.

The ease of persuading other people is directly tied to their current mental or emotional state. Someone who is lonely or tired is easier to persuade, simply because their defenses are lowered. Someone who is momentarily needy may be easier to persuade than someone who has a strong sense of self-worth. People who are at a low point in their lives are easy prey for others who might try to persuade them to do something they might not usually do.

The first step in persuasion involves the idea of reciprocating. If a person does something nice for someone else, then the receiving person usually feels the need to do something good in return. If someone helps their elderly neighbor carry in groceries from the car, that neighbor might feel obligated to bake homemade cookies for that person. A coworker who helps complete a project is more likely to receive assistance when it is needed. Many people do nice things for others all the time without expecting anything in return. The person who does nice things for people and then mentions some little favor that can be done in return may be someone to watch closely.

Nonprofit organizations use this tactic to gain more contributions to their causes. They will often send some little trinket or gift to prompt people to donate larger sums of money, or even just to donate where they might not have originally. The idea behind this is that the person opening the letter has received a little gift for no reason, so they might feel obligated to give something in return.

Some people are automatically tempted to follow authority. People in positions of authority can command blind respect to their authority simply by acting a certain way or putting on a uniform. The problem with this is that authority figures or those that look like authority figures, can cause some people to do extraordinary things they would not normally do had a person in a position of authority not been the one asking. And it is not simply held to people in uniform. People who carry themselves a certain way or speak a certain way can give the impression that they are something they are not.

For someone or something to be considered a credible authority, it must be familiar and people must have trust in the person or organization. Someone who knows all there is to know about a subject is considered an expert and is more likely to be trusted than someone who has limited knowledge of the subject. But the information must also make sense to the people hearing it. If there is not some semblance of accuracy and intelligence, then the authority figure loses credibility. Even the person who is acknowledged as an expert will lack persuasive abilities if they are seen as not being trustworthy.

The worst part of the power that goes along with persuasion is that things that are scarce or hard to get are seen as much more valuable. People value diamonds because they are expensive and beautiful. If they were merely pretty stones, they would not be as interesting. Inconsistent rewards are a lot more interesting than consistent rewards. If a cookie falls every time a person rings a bell, then they are less likely to spend a lot of time ringing the bell because they know the cookie reward will always appear. If, however, the cookie only appears sometimes, people will spend much more time ringing the bell just in case this is the time the cookie will fall.

There are ways to improve the power of persuasion. Just like any other trait, it can be made stronger by following a few strategies and by regular practice. Persuasion is a powerful tool in the game of life. Persuasive people know that they have an amazing power, and they know how to use it correctly. They know how to listen and really hear what other people have to say. They are very good at making a connection with other people, and this makes them seem even more honest and friendly. They make others feel that they are knowledgeable and can offer a certain sense of satisfaction. They also know when to momentarily retreat and regroup. They are not pushy. They are persuasive.

Did you know that your body speaks more eloquently than words? Body language is at work constantly whether you are aware of it or not. When you want to master the art of persuasion, you need not only understand (and read accurately) body language, but also learn to use it to drive your point home.

Body language is a mix of hand and facial gestures, posture and overall appearance. Using these to your advantage you can get people to do what you want without them realizing that you are actually controlling the outcome of the discussion.

Why people are persuasive

What makes a person convincing? Why are they persuasive, and you aren't? This is the answer we're going to pursue in this e-book, but I'm telling you now, there is no single, short answer to that question.

What makes this persuasive influence so difficult to pin down and elusive is precisely this almost mosaic quality it has. It's the result, the perfect merger of several important aspects that you wouldn't normally attribute to such an influence.

These aspects of their being don't only affect them, but affect us, as well. That's the fascination around it. It's all psychological, it's an overwhelming and sometimes unintentional psychological influence on the people around them.

Confidence is the absolute most important aspect when it comes to persuasion. There's no doubt it's been scientifically proven that it's easier to persuade people when you're confident. That's because it's just assumed you're an authority on the topic and they'll listen to you, because they have no knowledge or experience, but you seem to have both.

It's also crucial to understand that humans are doubtful creatures. We're not very confident and we don't really believe in our own abilities or even experience, so when someone comes along and appears to be confident and to know more, we follow them like a herd of dim sheep. Persuasion is just as much about the impression you leave upon people as it is about your actual skill. Like many other times in life, appearances are more "real" than actual reality, because it's all other people will ever know about you. It doesn't matter if deep inside, you're insecure or you don't really think you know what you're doing.

On the outside, you're this dazzling, confident creature that can persuade anyone into anything because you've mastered all the important contributing factors: confidence, eye contact, body language, manner of speaking, tone, facial expressions, as well as your general demeanor.

Confidence

How do you think so many scammers make a living? No, that sketchy guy selling you snake oil isn't really a doctor, but he speaks like he is one, so people believe him and throw money at him, genuinely believing he will solve their problems.

Now, I'm not advocating that you try to trick people, but I am telling you that you need to work on your confidence. You'll notice that every single person you find convincing has some sort of authoritative stance. It's like their presence demands attention and respect.

Eye contact

Eye contact is a classic, natural display of dominance. It's a technique that's even present in the animal kingdom, and if a lion doesn't intimidate you, I don't know who can. It's true that the goal isn't to intimidate? Eye contact can do that very effectively.

Body language

Do you know how often people underestimate body language, or just ignore it outright? I don't know why, because body language is an amazing tool for persuasion. People are always advised to display open body language, like facing your audience, making sure not to keep your arms crossed against your chest, keep your palms open, and all sorts of little tips that we'll discuss at length later.

What you maybe haven't heard is that in order to be effectively persuasive, you also need to take note of and use the body language of the person you're talking to.

Manner of speaking

Your choice of words is overwhelmingly important when attempting to convince someone, because it must be very deliberate. There's a clear strategy behind verbal persuasion, and it relies on appealing to the person's emotions.

The way you speak and what you say are both equally important, because even though your message may be perfect, if the delivery is lacking, it won't do much good. We've already established that speaking with authority is half the battle, but you also have to speak the right words, in order to win it.

Tone

Continuing on the idea that the way you say things is vastly important, let's talk about tone and why it matters. In fact, I lied when I said tone and message are equally important: tone weighs much more on a person's impression.

If someone has a very somber voice, a serious, measured tone, and an equally severe facial expression, it almost doesn't matter what they're saying – you're going to assume it's grave and important; the actual words or what they mean matters less. A joke told with a serious tone isn't funny at all.

Facial expressions

Facial expression goes hand in hand with body language and eye contact and is similarly important to tonality. Creating the impression that you mean what you say involves your face, because it will be the very first to betray you or, on the contrary, help you enforce your message.

General demeanor

Now, a lot of different aspects of your being can fall under "demeanor". General demeanor is actually one of the main things you need to master and it has one major rule: mirror the demeanor of the person you're trying to persuade.

Methods of Persuasion

Methods of persuasion can often be referred to under various terms, such as methods of persuasion and techniques of persuasion. Only one strategy can be used to convince somebody to think or act in some way. The agent may be able to speak to the subject when providing evidence to change the mind of the subject, may be able to use some kind of force or influence against the subject, and may be able to perform some kind of service to the subject, or use another tactic.

Usage of Force

The agent can decide that it is a good idea to use some force to convince the subject to think their way, depending on the situation. This can occur if the ideas don't fit together, daily dialogue doesn't work, or the agent gets irritated and unhappy with the conversation switch. Sometimes force is used as a form of scare tactic because it allows the subject less time to objectively think about what happens when a normal conversation takes place.

Typically force will be used when the agent is less effective using the other available means of persuasion, but sometimes it is often achieved beginning with the use of force. At other times, force can be used when the agent feels like they are losing control or when the subject may pose the agent with contradictory evidence and the agent is frustrated.

Weapons of Influence

One approach that can be used to convince the subject to lean a particular way is to use the available weapons of influence. Robert Cialdini has established these six forces.

Reciprocity

The principle of reciprocity is the first tool of power. This principle states that the subject should seek to repay the agent in kind if one person, the agent, provides the other person, the subject, with something of value. It basically means that when the agent performs some kind of service to the subject, the subject may believe that at some point they have an obligation to perform a service similar to the agent. While the two services may not be the same, they have the same value to match each other's obligation. The agent may be more likely to convince the subject to do or behave in some way because the subject will have that sense of duty hanging over them.

The added benefit to the agent's use of reciprocity is that it is not just a moral position which places the burden on the subject; it is also a standing held up by social codes.

Commitment and Consistency

Consistency is one of the persuasion process's most important aspects. This is because: Consistency is highly valued in society: most of the time people want things to stay that way. Consistency offers a very useful path through the complexities of modern life.

Social Proof

The subject will be affected by the people around them; they will be more likely to want to do what others are doing instead of doing their own thing. The subject will base their beliefs and behaviors on what others do about them, what they behave, and how they believe.

Liking

There are two key factors that will lead to the agent's preference for the subject. Physical attractiveness is the first, and similarity is the second.

For the first, if the agent is visually more appealing to the subject, they will have the impression of being more convincing as they can get more quickly what they want while also influencing others ' attitudes.

The second factor is a little better, similarity. The theory is that they are much more likely to answer in the affirmative to what the agent asks if the subject is similar to the agent. This mechanism is quite normal and most of the time the subject won't have to worry about if it's the right thing to do when they like it and are similar to the agent.

Authority

One way the agent can succeed in persuading the subject is by becoming an expert. Many people have a tendency to assume that something an expert says about a topic is real. The subject is more likely to enjoy listening to a trustworthy and competent agent; this means that if the agent can bring these two things to the table, they are already on the way to getting their subject to listen and believe them.

Scarcity

If the availability of a commodity or idea is limited, a higher value is more likely to be allocated. Consumers want more of what they can't have, according to Cialdini. The persuasion specialist will be able to take advantage of the notion of scarcity. They will have to find a way to make the subject think the item is unique by explaining why it is so different and what it does that nothing else can do. The agent will have to work in the right way on their subject.

What you can obtain through persuasion

Persuasion is a very powerful and very valuable skill that not everyone has, but that everyone should have. It comes in handy throughout your life in virtually any aspect of your existence, from sweet-talking your way into free movie tickets to convincing your boss you deserve a raise.

Your relationship with your spouse

Far from being unfair or manipulative, having the ability to convince your significant other can actually improve your relationship because you have fewer fights about your disagreements and lack of compromise. Now you can use all that extra time and energy implementing your superior decisions.

Your relationship with your kids

Having the persuasion skills and indisputable power and authority to convince your kids to actually do what you tell them to is as close to magic as you can possibly get. If you don't believe me, try it!

Your relationship with your friends

We all have that one friend who always makes terrible life choices and no one can get through to them and steer them towards the right path...except you, that is. If you have influence and persuasion skills, don't keep them for yourself. Use them for good, not evil.

Get paid what you deserve

Negotiating absolutely falls under persuasion, so really, absolutely everyone should have this skill. No matter if you're haggling at the market or discussing a higher salary, you need to have the ability to convince your 'opponent' that you deserve this and you should have it. It's mostly applicable in the workplace, where – let's be real – no boss will ever willingly part with their money and hand it over to you. So it's your job to convince them to do it. You've earned it, you deserve it, and it's rightfully yours. You have to ask for it, but you have to know how, and persuasive skills help with that.

Earn the trust and respect of your boss

You can accomplish that by becoming their go-to person. Offer your bright ideas, come up with solutions to problems the company is facing, persuade them to implement your suggestions and that they're the contribution the company needs right now. In time, you will reap the rewards when your boss comes to consult with your first.

Be a good leader to your colleagues

Obviously, your persuasive abilities will prove to be invaluable to a position like this if you want people to respect you, your work, and your ideas. It should be obvious for everyone that your way is the right way and there will be minimal dissent if you have the necessary influence over them.

Get out of paying tickets

Legally, a ticket is a mandatory consequence of breaking the law in some way, by speeding, failing to wear your seatbelt, talking on your cell while driving, etc. Practically, however...a ticket can be a negotiation, as long as you have the necessary skills.

Get into coveted clubs or restaurants

If you're persuasive enough, you can influence any menial gatekeeper and convince them to just let you through without needing to jump through fiery hoops or grease the well-meaning palms of anyone. Talk about some sweet perks!

Get important information

If you can talk the talk well enough, you can basically convince anyone to tell you anything. Gossip from your friend, preferred customer sales dates from sales attendants, where they keep the extra free peanuts from the flight attendant...you get the idea. Sweet talk yourself into perks and valuable info.

How to Persuade People

The ability to influence someone during a conversation and make a decision is necessary in order to become one of the most important people in the world today. This ability is useful in business negotiations, and in everyday life.

In general, the impact on people is not so obvious. The basic idea is that people's behavior is often guided by their subconscious simple desires. And to achieve your goals, you need to understand the simple desires of people, and then make your interlocutor passionately wish for something.

It should be noted that in order to influence people you should NOT try to impose or force them to make a hasty decision. It may seem incredible, but the person that wants to reach a mutually beneficial cooperation becomes a huge advantage compared to those that are trying to impose something on others. If you are willing to put yourself in the shoes of another person from whom you want to get something and understand his/her thoughts, then you do not have to worry about your relationship with the person.

The secret lies in the ability to help the self-affirmation of the interlocutor. It is necessary to make sure that your companion looks decent in his own eyes. First things first, there are six basic principles that will absolutely affect any of your interlocutors.

To achieve their goals, people often use the influence of psychology, which helps to manipulate man. Even in ancient times it can be seen that priests ruled the people, instilling in them that religion is harsh, and everyone will be punished if they cannot follow the established rules and practices. Psychological influence strongly acts on the subconscious, causing the victim being influenced to be led by a skilled manipulator.

If you want to succeed and learn how to manage people, these words of the great American entrepreneur should be your credo. You will grow your personality only when you are in close cooperation with the community. From childhood we develop the basic patterns of behavior and outlook, produced by the long historical, biological and mental development of humankind.

In order to have influence and control over another person, it is required that you know their personality and behavioral traits. Most importantly, learn how to use this knowledge to master the specific methods and techniques of influence and control the behavior of the other, on the basis of his outlook, character, personality type and other important psychological features.

If you want to learn how to manage people, secret techniques in this article will let you know not only the theoretical aspect of the question but also allow the use of this knowledge in real life.

To help people to look beyond the limits of consciousness, professionals use a variety of methods and techniques. One of the most effective of these is hypnosis. This method of direct influence on the psyche, whose essence consists of the introduction of human narrowed state of consciousness, makes it is easy to control someone else's suggestion and management.

The ability to manage people, primarily, is to combine the knowledge of human psychology and their personal characteristics. They help to change their own behavior so that this change will cause the desired reaction in others. Try to be more observant while communicating; it will help you better understand the individual psychological characteristics of the interlocutor. Based on this knowledge, try using the following methods and techniques that will help you manage people correctly and efficiently.

To learn how to manipulate people, you must know how it feels to be on both sides. After all, you need to understand the feelings and emotions experienced by each side. This section of the learning process will be much more efficient!

Just focus on the moral side of the issue. If you are ashamed to receive from people that are important to you, you do not accept selfish purposes - better close and do not hurt their highly moral consciousness of the information received.

Chapter 7 - Manipulations

Perhaps, one of the most interesting topics is connected with usage of manipulations in politics and society. Its principles are necessary to know otherwise you are at risk of appearing under somebody's dark games. Here we will talk how to understand manipulations listening to the conversations of politicians or mass media representatives.

As soon as politician starts using strange language adding some not really clear words, it is mostly done to make manipulations. If the speaker wanted everybody to understand him, he would explain clearly. After listening to such speeches, the audience complains of having blurred or foggy mind. Indeed, in our life, apart from professional areas of science and technologies, there are no problems which cannot be explained normally. Strange words pursue goal to press onto listener with false authority of expert or take a role of mesmerizing effect. They also can hide real lie. Thus, language is incredible important diagnostic tool to define manipulations.

Next, if politicians talk about emotions it is better not to react at their trembling voices or tearful eyes. When watching some TV-show or news you figure out excessive emotions which apply to our sense of being guilty or justice, you have to be completely sensible and pay attention only to the facts given. A person has to notice when he is under attack.

Sensation and urgency are technologies of common activity which cause total level of nervousness and undermine psychological protection. However, sometimes creation of artificial background of sensation serves some purpose and tries to distort your attention from real governmental problem. At the same time, authorities voted for law which increased retirement fees, and nobody noticed it being really excited about sensation.

Repetition is the main way of propaganda. Repetition causes some effect onto our subconsciousness what makes us really bad at controlling the process. For example, if well-educated national innovators put forward topic why sale and purchase of lands is absent, they never explain clearly why they need. It is good illustration of persuasion and repetition as no sensible reasons exist to prove the point of view while shadow social order has been accepted with money wasted onto their own needs. So, this is a real deception of nation!

Then, if politician is really eager to explain some problem widely, he will talk about it fully. However, manipulator will give us small piece instead of integral situation. He divides it into pieces to deprive us of possibility to analyze it adequately. Taking out of context means that politician has not spoken bout outer important factors, however, represents small detail as the crucial one. This is how stereotypes opinion is formed.

Unchangeable nature of decision is evidence of manipulation, too. Actually, our living process is flexible, and every step requires making choice mulling over it carefully. Nevertheless, when mass media tells us that there is no choice, and we need to follow the guidance, it is bad sign.

Mixture of information and opinion looks like that. In news it is stated that in Tokyo's underground somebody spilled poisonous substance, and then opinion is expressed that members of some sect are guilty. The next day information in mass media is given in such a way: 'Sect representatives who spilled poison in underground...' So, when there are too many opinionated expressions in the framework of news, a person has to remind himself that it might be manipulation.

Using reputation of famous person could bring a good reason why you act like that. For example, when investigator insists on necessity to use nuclear weapon for the sake of humanity and at the same time slightly reminds of being academic, it is real manipulation. His knowledge and scientific experience do not give him right to express such serious opinion concerning public decisions.

As well, we should always be suspicious when some politician or TV-host applies to our stereotypes evoking the sense of community and showing that we are better than others. So, how to behave while speaking with manipulator? The majority of people who know the theory of manipulation try to win over him using even dirtier techniques. However, the best advice which was ever given is to stop being with manipulator.

To sum up, let's identify top signs of political manipulations:

☐ insertion into consciousness of some information which is not objective at all, but oriented onto several social groups;

☐ making influence on painful points of consciousness which cause fear, panic, hatred, and anxiety;

☐ fulfillment of some intentions and hidden purposes with the help of total nation's approval.

Having finished talking about political manipulations, let us say that such tricks are stereotyped and used in all areas of relationships. Let's pay attention to how it works out in our daily life.

Women who have ever had addiction in relationships with the men could know themselves in the following list of crucial manipulator:

1. After the first date he insists on urgent meetings, overwhelms you with the great emotions, and it is almost impossible to have a break and think about his incentives. At this stage woman is getting used to

passion and regards it will last forever. If only she knew how much she was mistaken!

2. When the appropriate space for attachment is designed, he starts playing 'hot and cold' game. When you are sure he loves you so much, he disappears. As a result, most women begin to ruminate pondering question: 'What have I done wrong? Maybe, I have offended him?'

3. The worst moment is that manipulator is quite honest with you. He has never promised you anything. That's why you constantly analyze what he meant. He talks about love, however, relationships got stuck and apart from rare dates you are not proposed anything valuable.

4. His words have nothing in common with actions. Perhaps, at least once in a life you knew a person who promised to go for a walk with you at the weekend, invite at the birthday of the best friend or watch a new movie. However, right time for it never comes. He always has some reasonable explanation why this plan has to be postponed again and again.

5. He undermines your self-confidence. If you openly criticize him for not making promises, he will assure you haven't understood him properly. Then, you will appear as the selfish person who demands more than beloved one could give. He will develop these hesitations in you. The manipulator is accustomed to live here and now, he doesn't think about future. It is excellent strategy for him to enjoy the moment.

6. He is afraid of the word 'relationships'. Try to speak with him how he sees your future, and you are at risk of spoiling the meeting. He will try to convincingly tell how important it is to live now. If you continue insisting, he is likely to disappear.

7. You don't know his family and friends. Indeed, he speaks about them quite often causing an illusion that you have already met them. However, he does not hurry to invite you into the circle of his closest people.

8. Most of his friends are women. He represents them as good acquaintances. Such meetings cause suspicions which relationships they have. It is interesting that he maintains your ruminations making his personality incredibly important in your eyes.

9. He has never had long-term relationships. They separated not because he was guilty. Apart from that, he keeps talking that all the women he has ever met were villains or only needed his money. At the same time, he tries to emphasize that you are absolutely different person, that's why he spends time with you. At this point it is time to remember that once you have been raised at the place of unattainable angel, soon you will be taken down, and he will talk about you the same that you had heard about others.

Almost all the aforementioned reasons are relevant for the start of relationships, and they usually mean that a person is not willing to start living together or at least does not take you seriously. However, there are other examples of how men and women manipulate each other in the stable relationships making their partners totally attached.

Jane, 26: 'A man with whom I had been living for several years was father of my child. He used the only method called: 'Except for me, nobody needs you'. He convinced me that I was overweight and anybody could not have interesting conversations with me. Indeed, he criticized me a lot! Everything I did was wrong. At that moment I was twenty-three years old, and I believed in everything he told. I really considered him as the last hope in my life. My psychological addiction from him was broken when in some archeological expedition one young man gave me his coat because I could be frozen to death. Because of such reflection of warmth and open-hearted nature I cried my eyes out. When I understood how much I needed real love from my partner, I understood that nobody would be allowed to offend me anymore, and broke up with him. The funniest moment happened in a year after our separation. He sent me a letter where it had been written: 'Let's get married as nobody loved me like you did'. Honestly, I have never faced such a selfishness'.

Francesca, 30: 'My man attached me using my own psychological problems and weaknesses. Nowadays, after the divorce, he writes me messages from different countries where he is travelling using money from my apartment's sale. When we separated, during the next two years he continued asking for my car which had been bought several years before meeting him. In every message he used such phrases: 'You think only about money. I have never met anybody meaner than you are. You cannot love, all you need is money'. At the same time, for five years of living together he did not bring anything to our house. As well, he undermined my selfesteem by calling me fat and stupid. However, being twenty, I worked as model and made good money trying to find some finances for us and our child'.

As you see, the most typical manipulation in relationships is attaining partner by decreasing his selfesteem. It is done by using pseudo caring notices and actual afflictions. If you have faced such behavior from the side of your partner, it is moment of thinking. Phrases like 'Nobody will love you' or 'If it hadn't been for me, you would have had any achievements in this life' as well as collection of your disadvantages and comparison with others are the signs of manipulation. By the way, if the manipulator uses it consciously you will feel hardship trying to explain your own position to him. He will tend to subjection estimation and get you down to stereotypes, 'Everybody thinks so, don't be different'.

People who are susceptible to manipulations usually tend to have a kind of hole inside. They are not confident and try to find strong charismatic personality to approve their right for existence. After traumatic relationships they can get to religious cults because patterns used there resemble manipulation techniques.

In religion manipulations are connected with attempt to make everybody obey. Such phrases as 'All of us work for the sake of God', 'Are you going to argue with the blessing?', 'Where is your humbleness?' are examples of such mental techniques which can cause pain for a believer. After facing manipulations, some people disappoint in religion, others feel good about necessity to sacrifice your interests and have persuaded feeling of being guilty. Manipulations are not order or honest agreement. Their main feature is application to weaknesses and vulnerabilities which everybody has to get power over a person. The deepest level of manipulation is to change personal mindsets, replace his goals with different ones, manage his lifelong intentions, and orient him in a way we consider as right one. Desire to have power usually accompanies feeling of control, and both senses are attainable with the help of manipulations.

For example, if the priest tries to insure you that once you stop obeying some prescriptions, you will go to hell, it is real manipulation. The aim of this trick is to control the area of personal relations to revise the circle of acquaintances and all the aspects of life. Manipulation in religion and other scopes is based on the following feelings which have suffered since our childhood:

☐ Distorted understanding of love leads such a situation when good attitude appears after meeting the needs of manipulator; if you want to cope with such kind of technique, you should know that each person deserves love only because he was born. If a person behaves well with you only if you do what he wants, it is manipulation. Unfortunately, the religious principles of good and evil are based on this rule.

☐ Mythological religious stories are tools of making person obey. In case he does not want to do what is required, he is threatened to face troubles.

☐ Feeling of being guilty is another sign you have been manipulated. The object of bad influence has to explain his actions again and again. As a result, manipulator can promise to forgive him if some requirements are made.

☐ Lack of self-confidence is another place for manipulation. Perhaps, you know how painful it is to be pressed with somebody's reputation. Manipulator tries to convince that you are hopeless and helpless.

☐ Pride and vanity which might lead a person to career tops also can be used by the experienced manipulator. Flattery explain the necessity gives possibility to of committing some

actions illogical to make from the first glance. It is followed by the ambitious challenge to prove your success and supremacy.

☐ The feeling of pity causes desire to do everything instead of manipulator. At the same time, manipulator put responsibility on the shoulders of his victim by saying: "I will die without you".

☐ Hope is also exploited in such manipulative relationships. The victim believes that in case she will make everything as promised, award will be waiting for her. In situation with religion such an award is connected with life after death.

Here you should acknowledge the fact that all the stated manipulative tricks are used in all the areas of our everyday life. However, at the example of religion they look really illustrative. Before talking about the most widespread and breath-taking ways to manipulate others, let's ponder the next issue. So, how not to become a victim of such tricks? Actually, sensitivity towards manipulations appears in the childhood, when parents say they will love their child for good marks or clean house. A kid understands that he should meet his parents' expectations to deserve love. However, it is not true. A person whose childhood was full of unconditional love, more rarely reacts at manipulations. He has intuitive feelings that he always deserves the best attitude from the side of others. If he sees such manipulation, he has no desire to continue such communication because this pattern seems strange for him.

Chapter 8 - The Dark Triad

Personality Vulnerabilities

Manipulation predators or dark manipulators use a lot of techniques in order to control their victims. They look for a certain type of people with certain types of personalities. Those type of personalities that are often prey to manipulators are those with low or no self-esteem, those who are easy to please, those with low or no self-confidence, have no sense of assertiveness and are very naïve. Let's explain these personality traits in more detail.

Those who are naïve find it virtually impossible to accept the fact that particular people in their lives can be cunning, devious, and ruthless. They will constantly deny that they are being victimized.
Those who are over-conscientious give the manipulator the benefit of the doubt, even if they know in the back of their mind, they are right. They are hoping they are not and take the blame.
Those who have a low self-confidence start to doubt themselves and what they are experiencing, they are

not assertive and they easily defensive because they don't want to make waves.

Those who are emotional dependency have a submissive and dependent personality. When the victim is more emotionally dependent, the manipulator has an easier time exploiting and manipulating them.

Those who over intellectualize really want to believe the manipulator and tries to understand their reason for harming others, especially the victim themselves.

When people show signs of these characteristics, they are actually trying to get away with using others to get what they want. Each one of these personality traits can make life difficult for people, but all of these traits combined can be dangerous to anyone's mental health. Those who have any one of these personality traits show some of these behaviors: seeking out multiple sex partners, acts out aggressively to get what they want, they have high or low self-esteem, do not view themselves highly, and most of these traits are shown by men (Whitbourne, 2013).

It is important to note that people who have one of these three personality disorders are not trustworthy, are selfish, are not straightforward, are not kind, or modest, and they do not comply or compromise, which are all qualities that are not good for any type of relationship. If you know someone that exuberates any of the dark triad traits, you might want to see if you are a victim to any of these techniques.

Manipulation Techniques

Lying is one of the very first techniques that manipulators use. It is a technique that pathological liars or psychopaths use when they want to confuse their victims. If they are constantly lying to them, their victims will often be unaware of the truth. Those who use this tactic have no moral or ethical apprehension about it.

Telling half-truths or only telling part of a story is another tactic that can be used in order to manipulate someone one. People like this will often keep things to themselves because it puts the victim at a disadvantage. They can get what they want by waiting to tell them the rest of the story until their needs are met.

Being around someone who has frequent mood swings can often make a person vulnerable to their manipulations. Not knowing what mood that person will be in, whether they will be happy, sad, or angry can be a very useful tactic for the manipulator. It keeps the victim off balance and easy to manipulate because they will often do what the manipulator wants in order to keep them in a good mood.

Another tactic that is often used by narcissists is known as love bombing. This doesn't necessarily mean that you have to be a relationship. This tactic can be used in a friendship as well. Those that use this tactic will charm the victim to death and have them believe that this is the best relationship, friendship that has ever happened to them. They will use the victim for what they want, and then when they are done, they drop them, and the victim has no idea what happened.

A tactic that can be used in extreme cases by the manipulator is that of punishment. This makes the victim feel guilty for something they did wrong, even if they didn't do anything at all. Some of the punishments that they can inflict on their victim are consistent nagging, shouting, mental abuse, giving them the silent treatment, and even as bad as physical violence.

Denial is often a tactic that is used when a manipulator feels pushed in a corner, and they feel like they will be exposed for the fake that they are. In this instance, they will manipulate the victim into believing that they are not doing the very thing they are being accused of.

Spinning the truth is a tactic often used by politicians. It is used to twist the facts to suit their needs or wants. Sociopaths use this technique to disguise their bad behavior and justify it to their victims.

Minimizing is when a manipulator will play down their behavior and/or actions. They move the blame onto the victim for overreacting when their actions are actually harmful, and the person has a valid reason for feeling the way they do.

It is often interesting when the manipulator allows themselves to become the victim. They do this to gain sympathy or compassion from their real victims. They do this so that their victims feel a sense of responsibility to help and end their suffering, especially if they feel that they are the cause of that person's suffering.

Another way that the manipulator can move the blame onto the victim is through targeting the victim and accusing them of wrongdoing. The victim will them start to defend themselves, while the manipulator hides their own manipulation away from the victim. This can actually be dangerous because the victim is so focused on defending themselves that they forget to notice what is actually right in front of them.

Using the positive reinforcement tactic tricks the victim into thinking that they are getting something for helping the manipulator get what they want. This can be through purchasing them expensive presents, praising them, giving them money, constantly apologizing for their behavior, giving them lots of attention and buttering them up.

There are times when a person knows where they stand with someone. However, in any type of relationship, the manipulator might keep moving the goal just to confuse their victim because they thought that everyone was still on the same page.

Another manipulation tactic that manipulators like to use is known as diversion. This tactic is commonly used to divert a certain conversation away from what the manipulator is doing. The new topic is created to get the victim to lose focus on what the manipulator is doing or trying to do.

Sarcasm is a tactic that can be used to lower the self-esteem and confidence of a victim through embarrassment. The manipulator will use sarcasm – usually saying something about the victim- in front of other people. This gives the manipulator power over the victim because they just made them very small.

Guilt trips are another tactic that a manipulator will use against their victim. In this instance, they will often tell their victim that they don't care about them or love them; they will indicate that they are selfish and that their life is easy. It keeps the victim confused and anxious because they want to please the manipulator by letting them know that they care about them and will do anything for them.

Using flattery is the exact opposite of guilt tripping. In this instance, the manipulator will use charm, praise or other types of flattery to gain the victim's trust. They victim enjoys the compliments and lets their guard down.

Another way that a manipulator will move the blame is to play the innocent card when the victim accuses them of their tactics. They will act shocked or show confusion at the accusation. The act of being surprised is convincing to the victim, and it makes them question their judgment and if what they are feeling is wrong.

A dangerous tactic that a manipulator can use is that of extreme aggression. Rage and aggression are used to force the victim to submit. The anger and rage are a tactic that scares the victim to stop talking about the conversation. They pretty much want to help keep the manipulator's anger in check.

Isolation is another dangerous tactic used by manipulators. It is a control mechanism that is used by manipulators to keep their victims from their family, friends, and loved ones who can expose the manipulator for who they really are. The manipulator might know that their victim can be manipulated, but their friends and family are can see right through them, and they are not done using their victim yet.

And, one of the last tactics that manipulators, such as psychopaths and sociopaths use is that of fake love and empathy. These types of people do not know how to love others besides themselves and have a hard time loving others and showing empathy towards others. They use this tactic to entangle themselves into their victims lives in order to extract what they want from them (Learning Mind, 2012).

Remember that Dark Manipulation is a very dangerous thing and not something that anyone would want to be caught up in if they can help it. The more knowledge you have about these devious acts, the easier it is to protect yourself from it.

Chapter 9 - Mind Control

What is mind control? When people hear mind control, they immediately think of hypnosis or manipulation. These are both correct. We can also put brainwashing into this category. We will talk about all of these and how they can change our lives if we say yes to just the right person. When we talk about mind control, we are talking about persuasion, coercive persuasion, and mind distortion. This is the way that people can change our beliefs by changing their minds on topics. A lot of people put cults and cult leaders into talks about mind control. We will talk about Jim Jones in that regard.

In cults, the leaders will recruit followers. These followers will develop a very intimate relationship with the leader and the other cult members. This leader begins to abuse their power and start to manipulate the cult members into doing whatever they want. The cult leader is exploiting the members of the cult to get the power, money, or sexual pleasure that they want. They don't care who is hurt along the way. These cult relationships are often very destructive. We can see this in the story of Jim Jones and his cult.

Jim Jones is one of the most notorious cult leaders in history. He was born in Indiana in 1931. He began working as a faith healer and civil rights preacher. He would soon inspire many people to commit suicide based on his religious teachings. He studied the work of Stalin, Marx, Mao, and Hitler. He also read a lot of Gandhi's works, but clearly, he didn't do much with those teachings. He had a huge interest in religion and philosophy. He found that in religion, he found friends. He found people that accepted him for being weird, as some people called him.

Jones' father was affiliated with the KKK, and Jones felt that his father was his enemy because their views on racism were much different. Jim did not agree with his father's views, and this put them at odds for many years. Jim eventually married a woman named Marceline Baldwin. She was a nurse, and it was said that they were very much in love when they married. She stood by Jim's side through all of the Jonestown madness.

When Jones was 20, he decided that he wanted to start learning more about different religions and communities. He started going to Communist Party gatherings. This opened his mind to much more, and he decided to open his church to educate the people around him. This was when he went on to open the Peoples Temple. He continued to fight against racism and even won a humanitarian award for his help with racism.

Soon, more and more people would join the Peoples Temple, and Jones started to become excited about what this would do for the people. He traveled all over the world and started to recruit more and more members of his church. He preached about racial equality, and people were on board almost instantly. He was charismatic and charming. It was easy for people to follow him. Jones decided to build Jonestown in Guyana. This was when it all began to go downhill for him, his followers, and Congressman Leo Ryan.

Leo Ryan had been receiving letters that the people in Jonestown were not safe. Friends and relatives of the Jonestown members were scared for their loved ones' lives, and Ryan wanted to get to the bottom of this as soon as he could. He went to Jonestown with a camera crew, and what he found would shock him. He was met with open arms and even given a reception made for a king. Then, one of the members of Jonestown attacked him with a knife. Ryan got past the knifing and wanted to help members of the Temple get out. He took 15 members with him, and Jones said he would not stop them from leaving.

When Ryan and the members started to board a plane, Jones had his guards shoot them. Ryan was killed and four of the members who were trying to escape. That same day, the news spread the word of one of the biggest mass murders in history. There were 909 people who lived in Jonestown. There were 304 children. Jones had made a special drink for them all to ingest. It was grape Flavor Aid that was laced with cyanide. He wanted all of his church members to commit what he called "revolutionary suicide." Children were given this drink first, and then the parents would drink it as they watched their children die. Jones had such mind control over his followers that they all died in his name. This is the type of mind control that predators have over their victims. He knew how to make people say "yes" to him no matter what the consequences.

Is there a difference in mind control and brainwashing? It has been used in cults, prisons, and abusive relationships. It is a way to change what someone is thinking by using techniques to get them to change their mindset. It can change their emotions, their actions, and their decision-making skills. It can also change their behaviors. This is a full process that people work on for quite a long time. It is not something that happens overnight.

How is mind control different than brainwashing? Mind control is different because the predator here is usually considered to be a close friend or helper. The victim already knows them. In brainwashing, the victim does not know the predator. This is why brainwashing is more common in cult settings than in relationship or marriage type settings. What is interesting about cult leaders is that they never feel as if they are brainwashing or trying to control anyone. They feel that they do not torture their cult members, and they never force a person to do anything that is against their will. These leaders tell their members to make their own choices but do so based on the beliefs of the cult.

Mind control is another way that predators try to make decisions for their victims based on what they want out of it. There are many ways to determine if someone is controlling you. People everyday use mind control, and you never know if someone has a plan to use it on you. There are some ways to tell if someone is trying to use mind control on you, though. The first way is through isolation. Do you feel that your partner is trying to isolate you from your family and friends? This is a sure sign that they are trying to control you. This person may want you all alone and all to themselves.

When your partner is constantly sulking and making you feel bad about it as if it is your fault, they could be using mind control on you. When they start to do this, you probably change your behavior almost instantly. They want you to change, and this is a sign that they want to control your mind. Lastly, do they make rules for you and your lifestyle? Do they try to keep you from seeing your friends? Do they give you specific times and a regular schedule that you are to follow? This is a sign that they are using mind control on you.

There are some ways that you can avoid being controlled like this, though. No matter what this person is saying to you about your family, always stay close to them. If you need to change their names on your phone, do it. It is important that if you feel that you are being controlled, you can get out of the situation. Your family can help you to do so. If your partner is sulking around and getting angry at you for actions that you didn't do, walk away from this situation. It may not be easy to get out, but if you stay close to friends and family, they can help you out of it.

Have you thought of what it would be like to mind control people? There are ways to do it, but we hope that if we give you this advice, you will not use it to hurt someone you care about. There are ways that you can use and get people to help you. These are not wicked ways to use mind control to show you how it is done.

Mind control isn't like magic, and it isn't about being a cult leader. It is actually about how well we market ourselves. This can come in handy if you are in the world of sales or politics. You can learn how to market yourself and lead your followers to believe in you and your products. You have to study their personality and let them think for you. This may sound silly, but it does work. It is important that if you are selling something never to tell a person to "think on it." People have way too much to think about already, and this can cause a problem with your sale. These people do not put your item or selling technique at the top of their lists, and then they forget about you. In mind control, you will have to think for them. Giving them the option to think it over is not helping your case.

Just do all of the legwork for them. Set it all up, and all they have to do is sign the dotted line. For example, if you want your new customers to give you a rating, instead of asking them to do it over and over again, send them emails about the best ways that they can write a review for you. This will be an easy way to get them to do it, and you can even make it a copy and paste form, so they don't have too much work to do. Another way to mind control people is to have a deadline that is real. If you tell people that you are almost sold out of a product, chances are they will commit to buying it from you. If you tell them that your sale is over today, there is another chance they will buy. If the sale isn't up yet or you still have thousands of that product, they don't have to know that. This is just your way of mind-controlling them into buying what you are selling. If they see your sense of urgency, they will act on it sooner because they know that they are getting in on a great deal!

When you study someone's personality and their mind, you get to see all kinds of angles of them. You will get to sense their emotions and one of the easiest ways to mind control someone is to get to their emotions and try to engage them. If you are selling something that smells good, try to find that memory they have of that scent. Take this memory and add it in with one of yours. For example, if you are selling rose soap and they tell you that their grandmother always used that scent, find a way to describe the way you feel when you smell a soap that your grandmother used. You will be surprised how quickly their emotions will change when they know the two of you have something like that in common. They are more likely to buy that from you as well.

Chapter 10 - Hypnosis As A Form Of Mind Control

Hypnosis is something that many people consider to be fake or a myth. Many skeptics don't take it seriously, but others think that hypnosis is another form of mind control. Hypnosis is a type of legitimate therapy used for many patients. Some patients will use it to stop overeating, while others will use it to stop smoking. Many people do misunderstand it and its uses because it is not used everywhere and on everyone. There is medical research that has shown that it can work and it can be used in therapy.

Some people view hypnosis as the man waving the clock back and forth and saying, "you are getting very sleepy." This is an old image of how hypnosis used to be done, and there are new ways that it is done today by therapists. Hypnosis is used to make suggestions to the patient who is looking for help. This is why many think of it as a type of mind control. The power of suggestion can help people think just about anything they want, and we saw that in the Jim Jones case.

As a treatment option, hypnosis helps people to treat their problems and cope with issues that they have. The therapists will make slight suggestions on how they can do this while they are under hypnosis. Patients are put in a trance-like state, and this is when the therapist will start to give them suggestions on making their lives better. When you are under hypnosis, your brain goes through some changes. There are two major areas that are affected during hypnosis. These two places in the brain help you to process and control the things happening inside of your body. When your therapist tells those parts of the brain to stop eating whenever you're bored, the brain takes this information and moves it around your entire body. This is how hypnosis can work and be a great way to treat grief or other ailments. Many people will use hypnosis when nothing else has worked for them.

Many people believe that hypnosis is a type of mind control. This mind control comes in the form of suggestions. These suggestions can be verbal or non-verbal, and we will dive into each of these to show you what is done in hypnosis. We will start with verbal hypnosis and the suggestions made during a session. Verbal hypnosis is also known as conversational hypnosis. This type of hypnosis is a way to communicate with someone's unconscious mind. This is also done through a conversation with a patient. Verbal cues in this type of hypnosis include using some keywords that will unfasten the mind. Depending on what secrets the patient is holding, this could end up pretty dangerous, especially if the patient doesn't want these secrets coming out. This is why many people do not trust going to a verbal hypnotist.

Verbal hypnosis also uses vague words and phrases to try and get more out of the patient. This type of hypnosis has occurred in history with leaders and rulers all over the world. When these patients were given cues, they exposed more than they ever thought that they would! This type of hypnosis may have you a bit worried, but if you are going to a therapist to be hypnotized, you are perfectly safe. Never let someone hypnotize you unless they are a trained professional. There is a non-verbal way to practice hypnosis as well. You probably guessed that this type of hypnosis is done without conversation. The eyes are what is used the most in this type of hypnosis. This is the type that many people will associate with mind control. The eyes are said to link the patient with the hypnotist, and this can help the patient get through their problems. A lot of people are not sure if they should trust this type of hypnosis because it is not used very often.

Hypnosis Tactics

When trying to hypnotize someone, there are many tactics that the hypnotists will use. We will explain these to you and show you just how they could be in the realm of mind control. One of these is called NLP, or neuro-linguistic programming. This is a type of hypnosis that is unlike anything traditional. In NLP, our behaviors are said to be associated with all of the sensory experiences that we have had. NLP focuses on olfactory, gustatory, auditory, visual, kinesthetic, and digital.

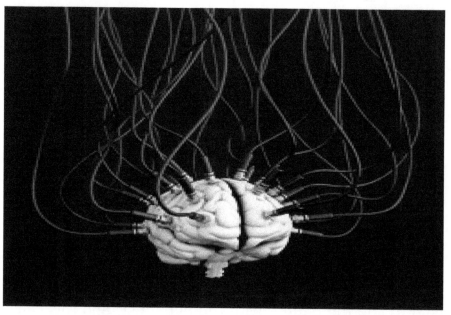

There are a few basics in NLP. First, there is a focus on ambiguity and the power it holds for us. For example, those who practice NLP will say things that help the patient with the best and most useful content for them at this very moment. The therapists will say, "do what is right for you" instead of telling them exactly what to do. There is a rhythm and tonality to NLP, along with a good and even flow. NLP therapists will use a lot of sounds to help their patients. They also use different language patterns with their patients, and that helps to change the commands that they are giving when their patient is in their trance-like state.

The tones that are used all have different meanings. The voice is giving commands, instead of asking questions. The command is given more emphasis, and the voice is changed when it is more important. The voice gives the patient a full reflection and meaning of the words that the therapist is using. There is non-verbal communication used in NLP, but the therapists will generally use their voice to give commands.

Anchoring is another popular tactic that is used in hypnosis. When an anchor is used, this means that the therapist is using a living memory to make an association with the patient. These anchors can be made of any senses, and when an anchor is used, therapists notice that the life memory becomes stronger as the senses are added in. An example would be mentioning a word like "daisy." Some people will see the flower, while there are others who may see a pet or a woman. They may have fond memories of the flower, and this helps them to make the association and get the life memories more vivid in the therapy session.

There are some things to understand about using an anchor, though. Sometimes an anchor can trigger bad memories for a person. This is when you need to explain to them that their life memory is meant to be a safe place and not something that brings them pain. You must be able to understand just how intense the anchor you are using is. Your timing needs to be right as well. If you use an anchor for someone during a bad time for him or her, the hypnosis may go the opposite direction that you want it to. You will also need to figure out if any of the senses they used are a direct correlation to a trigger or stimulus for them. This is key when you are working with an anchor.

To make their patients feel as if they have a safe place, they let them get into their favorite position to relax in. If they are not comfortable in the office, the therapist can suggest other options for them. Many patients with severe triggers like to spend their therapy sessions outside and feeling the fresh air. The therapist will also ask a string of questions that will help them to determine what the patient's triggers are. This will help them to determine what senses they will try and stimulate and what anchor to use.

There are a few principles that therapists use when they put anchors into their sessions. The first is trust and interpersonal absorption. This is making sure that the trust of the patient is secured. This needs to happen before there is any anchor applied to the sessions. This may take one visit or many. If the patient stays with the therapist, then they can determine that trust is locked in. Uniqueness is also a part of the therapy. This means that anchors will be linked to the therapists, and they will have to be anchors that are not ones that bring up triggers or life memories for them. They are only to bring up life memories for the patients. This can be tricky for a therapist, so it is best for them to bring up the unique anchors they can produce. This does take a lot of work on the therapist's part as well.

Reframing is another tool that therapists use when they are with patients who are being hypnotized. This is a way to get them to look at a situation differently. It seems like many therapists do this anyway, so what makes it so different in hypnosis? Many therapists call this positive reframing because they are trying to get their patients to have a more optimistic view of their life and what has happened recently in their life. Many will try to do this after their patients have had a death in their family or a traumatic event has occurred. When reframing is used, it doesn't change the situation for the patient. It just helps them to reduce the damage that has been done already. It will put the situation in a different perspective, and it is usually a healthier way for them to look at it. Many therapists will try to use this technique to break the ice with their patients and try to add humor into their sessions. Those with open minds will love this type of therapy, but some do not want to add humor into their sessions until they feel better from their grief or sadness.

Lastly, we have the future pacing technique. This is a way that therapists will use the anchor in the sessions and connect other changes and resources to it. When you hear the words mental imagery, this is a type of it. Future pacing generally will happen at the end of an NLP session and helps to guarantee that the changes made in the patient's mind are feasible in the outside world. Future pacing is used only when patients possess certain traits. When a patient is calm, their breathing has slowed, and their blood pressure is then therapists can use this technique. Much like anchoring, if future pacing is used at the wrong time, there could be triggering effects that could do damage to the patient. When future pacing is used, the therapist will think about a few things. First, they will think about all of the different situations for the future for their patient. They will use the senses to explain to the patient how to change their current situation. They will also talk to their patient about the positive changes that this will have on their lives. They will also walk them through the many ways that they can respond to any sudden changes in their lives.

All of these techniques can be used in hypnosis. If you feel that you want to try it, we suggest finding a professional who can walk you through it step by step. It is important to check their credentials and read the reviews. If you know someone close to you who has used a hypnotist, ask for their opinion and if it did work for them.

Chapter 11 - How To Use Dark Psychology In Your Daily Life

People use psychology within their daily lives, so why not use dark psychology and the tactics to protect yourself in everyday life. There are quite a few personality traits that can be very harmful if you get caught up in them. Sadists fall under this category. For instance, this personality type enjoys inflicting suffering on others, especially those who are innocent. They will even do this at the risk of costing them something. Those who are diagnosed as sadists feel that cruelty as a type of pleasure, exciting and can even be sexually stimulating. This is why they are a trait that people need to watch out for.

We do have to face the fact that we manipulate people and deceive people on a daily basis. When it comes to deception, people are deceiving not only others on a daily basis, but they are also deceiving themselves. People often lie to gain something or to avoid something. They might not want to be punished for an action, or they might want to reach a goal, and they self-deceive to get there.

Here are some examples of how people can deceive themselves on a daily basis:

Having a hard time study- this is a common occurrence. When people are trying to study, they find a lot of things that can distract them, especially cell phones and social media apps. They will find just about anything to distract them from the task at hand. These types of people seem to have a phobia of not studying long or well enough and they are afraid that they will come home with a bad grade and it will show how unintelligent they are. So, they take the art of self-deception and come up with the idea that will help prevent them from studying. This excuse will weigh better in their mind if they do end up getting a bad grade on their test. The person's subconscious is basically telling them that it is better for them to get bad grades for lack of studying, than to get them and having to blame their intelligence. They couldn't live with that.

Here are other ways that we deceive ourselves on a daily basis:

Procrastinating – People often waste time when they do not want to study or do something important. However, the main reason for procreating could be the phobia against failing and procrastinating was just an excuse. Self-confidence can be an issue as well.

Drinking, doing drugs and carrying out bad habits - People often fall into bad habits, drink or do drugs just to have something to blame if they fall again. This type of people will try to convince themselves that if they could stop doing drugs, they could be very successful. When they are the ones deceiving themselves and standing in their own way.

People often hold back because life is unfair. They tell themselves that we all live in a big lie that most people believe in, but not them. It is easier to blame it on life being unfair, then hold ourselves accountable for not reaching our goals.

If you realize that you have been deceiving yourself, here is a couple of things that you can do to change that.

Remember that you are actually really smart and the fact that you have been able to deceive yourself reaffirms it. If you were not smart, there would have been no way that you would have been able to come up with some of those ideas.

It is really important to learn how to face your fears. If you are running from a certain trauma, or not wanting to take a test, you have to remind yourself that you are stronger than this and that you can beat it.

Lastly, once you face your fears, your self-confidence and courage will grow.

Manipulation in our daily lives

Manipulation is an underhanded tactic that we are exposed to on a daily basis. Manipulators are people who want nothing more than to get their needs met, but they will use shady methods to do so.

Those who grew up being manipulated, or being around manipulation, find it hard to differentiate between what is really going on because if you are experiencing it again, it might actually feel familiar. Maybe the current relationship that you are in reminds you of your childhood.

This is important because manipulation tactics break apart communication and break peoples trust. People will often find ways to manipulate the situation and play games rather than speaking honestly about what is actually going on. However, there are others who value communication only to manipulate the situation to reveal the weaknesses of the other person, so that they can be in control. These types of people do this on a daily basis in conversation. They have no concern with listening to others talk about anything about themselves. And they are not there to help those people get through whatever it is that they are going through. It is all about dominance in this case and that's it.

Here are some of the tactics that can be used on an everyday basis:

. Some of the normal everyday techniques that we can experience are:

Lying – White lies, untruths, partial or half-truths, exaggerations, and stretching the truth.
Love Flooding – Through endless compliments, affection or through what is known as buttering someone up.

Love Denial – telling someone that they do not love you and withhold your love or affection from them until you get what you want.

Withdrawal – through avoiding the person altogether or giving them the silent treatment.

Choice Restriction – Giving people options that distract them from the one decision that you don't want them to make.

Reverse Psychology – Trying to get a person to do the exact opposite of what you want them to do in the attempt to motivate them to do the direct opposite, which is what you really wanted them to do in the first place.

Semantic Manipulation – Using common words that have a mutual definition with a person and later telling them that you have a different view of the conversation that you just had.

Being Condescendingly Sarcastic or Having a Patronizing Tone – To be fair, we are all guilty of doing this once in a while. But those who are manipulating us in conversation are doing this on a consistent basis. They are mocking you; their tone indicates that you are a child, and they belittle you with their words.

Speaking in Universal Statement or Generalizations – The manipulator will take the statement and make it untrue by grossly making it bigger. Generalization are afforded to those who a part of a group or things. A universal statement is more personal.

→ Example: Universal Example: You always say things like that.

→ Example: Generalization: Therapists always act like that.

Luring and Then Playing Innocent – We, or someone we know, is good at pushing the buttons of our loved ones. However, when a manipulator tries to push the buttons of their spouse and then act like they have no idea what happened. They automatically get the reaction that they were after and this is when their partner needs to pay close attention to what they are doing. Those who are abusive will keep doing this again and again until their spouse will start wondering if they are crazy.

Bullying - This is one of the easiest forms of manipulation to recognize. For example, your spouse asks you to clean the kitchen. You don't want to, but the look they are giving you indicates that you better clean it or else. You tell them sure, but they just used a form of violence to get you to do what they wanted.

Later they could have told you that you could have said no, but you knew you couldn't. It is important to note that if you fear that you cannot say no if your relationship without fearing for your safety, then you need to leave the relationship.

Using Your Heart Against You – Your spouse finds a stray kitten and wants to bring it home. The logical thing to do, would be to have a discussion about being able to house and afford the cat. But instead, they take the manipulative approach. Their ultimate goal is to make you feel bad about not being able to take care of the animal. Don't let anyone, even your spouse, make you feel that you cannot make the best choice for you. You do not have to take care of the kitten if you don't want to. Bottom line. Meet their manipulations with reasonable alternatives.

"If you love me, you would do this" – this one is so hard because it challenges how you feel about your spouse. They are basically asking you to prove your love for them by giving them what they want from you, making you feel guilt and shame. The thing you can do in this instance is to stop it altogether. You can tell your spouse that you love them without having to go to the store. If they wanted, you to go they could just ask.

Emotional Blackmail – this is ugly and dangerous. The idea that someone will harm themselves if you leave them is harmful at the core. They are using guilt, fear, and shame to keep having power over you. Remember that no one's total well being is your responsibility alone. You have to tell yourself not to fall for it. This will always be a manipulation tactic. However, you can tell them that you if they are feeling like they are going to harm themselves that you will call an ambulance to help them.

Neediness When it's Convenient – Has your spouse started to feel sick or upset when they didn't get what they wanted? This is a direct form of manipulation. For instance, they don't want to go somewhere with you and have a panic attack, that you have to help them through, so that they don't have to go at all. This is not healthy at all, and if this persists you should think about ending it

They Are Calm in Bad Situations – When someone gets hurt, or their conflict, somebody dies, your spouse always seems to not react with any feeling. They are always calm. This type of manipulation makes you think that may be how you are reacting is a bit much. Maybe your emotions are a little bit out of control. This is a controlling mechanism because no one should be able to tell you how to feel. This might seem like they are questioning your mental health and maturity level, and you find yourself looking to them and how to respond in certain situations. If this something that happens often and you see that you keep falling for it, you might need to go and see a therapist. This way, they can help you work on your emotional responses and find your true ones again. This manipulation method can be very damaging to your psyche. At the moment, learn to trust your gut. It will not steer you wrong.

Everything is a Joke – This is a two-part manipulation tactic. Your spouse will say hurtful things about you, and then when you get upset, they get upset because you can't take a joke. Other times they will joke about you in front of others, and if you don't respond in a positive way, you are again ruining the fun. This is a way to put you down continuously without having to take responsibility for it. Remember that you are not ruining the fun here, but you have to stand up for yourself.

Forcing Their Insecurities On To You – Your spouse will manipulate you into thinking that their insecurities are now your problem and will use them in a way to control you. They will tell you that they have been cheated on before, and that's why they don't like that you have male friends and that you should stop. Or they use them when they act a certain way, controlling your behavior because they don't want to lose you. When it comes to this situation, you have to find a balance. You can care for someone and make sure that you are considerate of their feelings, but you should not be manipulated into feeling what your spouse wants you to feel. Their manipulation is ruled by guilt.

Makes You Responsible and Accountable for What He/She Feels – This manipulation tactic is quite funny because your spouse spends a great deal of time making you think and feel like you cannot think about your or their feelings on your own, but that you have to be reminded of how they feel. They tell you how you feel, and then you are responsible for how they feel. If they're sad, you made them sad. You must have done something to make them feel that way. This tactic belittles you also because they take a lot from you and tell you how you feel, but then they want you to be responsible for how they feel.

Makes You Want What They Want, and Makes You Believe That Too – We all make compromises in relationships. However, what is not normal is having to put aside what you want completely to appease your spouse so that you can fully commit to what they want. If you soon start to see that your spouses' needs are being met far more often than yours, you need to start questioning things. You need to ask yourself if you are giving them what they want because you want to, or because they made you feel guilt or a sense of responsivity for how they feel? If you find that you are giving up everything for them, then you need to reconsider what is really important.

When determining how to get away from those who manipulate you on a daily basis, it is important to know your fundamental human rights and how you should not be treated.

You have the right:

To be respected and treated with respect.
To express how you feel, your opinions and the things you want and need.
To set your own priorities and goals.
To say no and not feel guilty about it.
To get what you pay for without guilt or shame.

That it is okay to have an opinion that is different from those in the group.

To stand up for yourself.

To take care of yourself.

To protect yourself from being threatened or harmed psychically, mentally and emotionally.

And, to create your own life full of happiness.

These specific rights help you set important boundaries that will help protect you in the future. We do have to remember that there will be people in this world who do not respect these rights or us as people, just things they can use to move on to the next phase. Do not let others take over you and manipulate your life. You are the only one who has power and authority over your life. And you are the only one who is in charge of it too.

Keep your distance from those who you think are trying to manipulate you or others. See how they act when they are around different people in different situations.

Avoid blaming yourself even though it is common to feel that way when someone is trying to expose your weaknesses and use them for their own personal gain. You have to keep telling yourself that you are not the problem and that they are trying to get you to surrender your power. If this occurs, ask some very basic questions: is my spouse treating me with respect? Are they reasonable with me? Do I feel good about myself while in the relationship? And, finally is this relationship going two ways or one?

If you answer negatively to all of these questions, then you know that you are not in a good relationship because you are going to continue to keep being manipulated from someone who tells you that they care, but they really don't. Once you realize that, you will be better off.

Manipulation can be a tactic that you are not aware of until someone points it out or you start connecting the dots. Often times, people figure it out when they are already stuck in a situation that is dangerous to get out of. With this being said, try to get to know people before you invest time in them. This is easier said than done because people don't usually reveal their true nature, especially those who mean to do you harm until you have already invested a lot of time with them. If you find that you feel uncomfortable and start to question what is going on. You should listen to your gut and move on. Everyone deserves to be happy.

Chapter 12 - Create a Foolproof Façade

If you are using Dark Psychology, then you have a dark side. But don't feel bad. All people have a dark side. Some people just suppress that side and don't explore all of the power that it has to offer. You, on the other hand, have decided to explore and even enrich your dark side. Many benefits await you. Human beings are naturally ruthlessly competitive creatures. The only ones who succeed are people who are willing to violate morals and ethics to get to the top. Now that you have decided to do this, you will get to the top, too. You will only fall behind and lose at life if you don't become cut throat and shameless about going after what you want. But in our society, we have to at least pretend to follow the current social code of morals and ethics. Otherwise, people will judge us harshly and avoid us. They won't be as willing to like you and to help you out. Your Dark Psychology training will no longer work if people start to dislike you and avoid you. Therefore, you must create a façade that totally obscures your dark side. You must hide behind an elaborate and beautiful façade that fools people into liking and trusting you. It is the only way to get away with Dark Psychology.

So how do you create this lovely, warming façade that fools the world? How are you supposed to look to others? How do you hide what you are really up to? How do you make people believe that you mean only the best, and that you are not ruthless and self-serving? Well, deception is part of it. But so is denial. And so is confidence. You can create a very convincing façade if you blend these three elements into your outward projection of yourself. A façade so convincing that you will have everyone fooled.

Deception

It's OK to lie about yourself and present yourself deceptively if it builds your image. You can use deception to make yourself look good to others. Just make sure that your lies are not blatant. You want to mislead people by making yourself look good, but you don't want to lie and look pathetic should you get found out. Always tell at least most of the truth when you talk about yourself.

Let's say you are on a date. You want to make the best impression but you don't have a great job. You don't want to lie outright about your job as you might get caught. Instead, talk up your job and use words that exaggerate the importance of your position.

Focus on your strengths when you speak about yourself, too. Try to show off your strengths. Don't show off your weaknesses. Downplay your weaknesses to make yourself look better. The better your outward image is and the more positive of a character you appear to have, the more people will like you. Then you will have better luck with people.

Denial

Denial can help you appear innocent. There are many aspects to denial. You should combine deception and denial in order to fool people into thinking that you are incapable of wrongdoing.

In the chapter on manipulation, we talked about the victim card. This is a good one to play. Deny that you have ever done wrong and pretend to be an innocent victim to justify your actions.

You can also pretend that you didn't know what you did was wrong. You made an honest mistake. Now, you're repenting and consumed with guilt. Deny that you are immoral and pretend to be the grieving sinner. People will feel that you have a good heart, even if you have messed up in the past. They will forgive you and admire you for your brevity.

You can also just flatly deny that you have done what others say about you. Act shocked when you hear stories about yourself. Then tell people some stories of your own to discredit those who talk badly about you. Deny that you had any involvement in any wrongdoing in the past.

Confidence

Confidence is the key to creating an innocent and believable façade. In fact, confidence is the key to getting others to like you. People are attracted to those who possess healthy confidence and ego. If you project confidence, you will draw people to you. And then your façade will definitely work.

Have you noticed that vain, narcissistic people are usually the most popular and well-liked? This is because they are totally confident and don't let others ruffle their feathers. Basically, they have such thick skins that nothing can stir up their insecurities. They are bold and passionate about who they are and what they want. You need to become this way.

Confidence is not just something that you must possess. You can fake it. Faking it will actually make you confident over time. And you can convince others that you possess lots of confidence, even if you really don't. Start acting confident today. It all lies in body language and speech. If you walk with a straight spine, look people in the eyes, and speak first, you will appear far more confident. You should also speak very directly and avoid stuttering or being inarticulate. Doing this will make you appear like you have nothing to hide and nothing to be ashamed of, which will inspire trust and admiration in others. This is partly why confidence is so attractive. You may also establish dominance over others by being confident, which gives you that authoritative edge that is so beneficial in persuasion. You can also take being confident a bit farther. Being cocky may go against your nature and your sense of modesty, but it's really the best way to charm people. Yes, people claim that they are put off by cocky people, yet look who gets the most women or men. Being cocky is not the same as being confident. But it can work for you. Putting on a charmingly cocky façade is a great way to make people feel attracted to you. They won't know why, but they will feel inexplicably drawn to your suave and vain nature. Be sure to brag about yourself, while also complimenting others. Shamelessly talk to people, forcing your nature on them and never taking no for an answer. Don't ever speak doubtfully or belittle yourself.

Confidence also helps you justify what you do to yourself. If you believe that you are a great person who deserves the best and that there is nothing wrong with what you are doing to others, then you won't give away your secret dark side out of guilt, doubt, or hesitation. You will simply act on your desires boldly and shamelessly. You will think that you are doing nothing, and thus you will act like you are doing nothing wrong. Shockingly, people will believe you more often than not if you act like you are in the right.

Conclusion

In closing, Dark Psychology is still in its infancy in terms of studying it and learning from it—and learning from the people, the Dark Personalities, who live there. It's not a fun place, but as Delroy Paulhus seems to feel, hanging out with a Psychopath or a Machiavellian would certainly be more interesting and maybe even more fun at times than spending the weekend with an agoraphobic.

And make no mistakes, these Dark Triad/Tetrad characters, they've been with us since we were upright. They may be dangerous at times, and wreak havoc and cause damage, but they also contribute to whatever society they're a part of. And they're a part of every society. And contributing to a society's well-being, not just to its darker sides.

Take Dan Mallory, for instance. He's the best-selling author of the debut thriller, The Woman in the Window. Bright, young, talented, successful—and very likely a Psychopath. In a New Yorker profile from February 2019 titled "Unreliable Narrator," coworkers describe him in Dark terms. Not dark Dark. But dark enough, disturbing enough, questionable enough, that it earned him more of an expose than a profile in a major American magazine. Psychopathic. Guilty of gaslighting. Narcissistic. Dark enough that he could easily serve as a textbook case in the annals of Dark Psychology.

If there's any doubt that these Dark Personalities are out there, among us, in the public eye, even serving as role models of sorts, Mallory's presence, and popularity, shows just how maddening, and maddeningly fascinating, these Dark Personality types can be. And how they still have plenty to teach us—about ourselves, about what makes people tick, what makes them behave the way do, what makes them think they can behave so darkly. And get away with it. Which they often do.

CPSIA information can be obtained
at www.ICGtesting.com
Printed in the USA
LVHW011703220221
679517LV00004B/191